T0339553

GRAPHIC

Today, almost anyone can upload and disseminate newsworthy content online, which has radically transformed our information ecosystem. Yet this often leaves us exposed to content produced without ethical or professional guidelines. In *Graphic*, Alexa Koenig and Andrea Lampros examine this dynamic and share best practices for safely navigating our digital world. Drawing on the latest social science research, original interviews, and their experiences running the world's first university-based digital investigations lab, Koenig and Lampros provide practical tips for maximizing the benefits and minimizing the harms of being online. In the wake of the global pandemic, they ask: How are people processing graphic news as they spend more time online? What practices can newsrooms, social media companies, and social justice organizations put in place to protect their employees from vicarious trauma and other harms? Timely and urgent, *Graphic* helps us navigate the unprecedented implications of the digital age while staying engaged with the human struggles of our times.

Alexa Koenig is Co-Director of the University of California, Berkeley's Human Rights Center and Adjunct Professor at UC Berkeley School of Law. She co-founded the Human Rights Center Investigations Lab and is an author of *Hiding in Plain Sight* (2016) and *Digital Witness* (2020).

Andrea Lampros is the Communications Director at the University of California, Berkeley School of Education. She is the former Associate Director at the Human Rights Center, co-founder of the Human Rights Center Investigations Lab, and the former Resiliency Manager of the lab.

Graphic

TRAUMA AND MEANING IN OUR ONLINE LIVES

ALEXA KOENIG

University of California, Berkeley

ANDREA LAMPROS

University of California, Berkeley

CAMBRIDGE
UNIVERSITY PRESS

Shaftesbury Road, Cambridge CB2 8EA, United Kingdom

One Liberty Plaza, 20th Floor, New York, NY 10006, USA

477 Williamstown Road, Port Melbourne, VIC 3207, Australia

314–321, 3rd Floor, Plot 3, Splendor Forum, Jasola District Centre, New Delhi – 110025, India

103 Penang Road, #05–06/07, Visioncrest Commercial, Singapore 238467

Cambridge University Press is part of Cambridge University Press & Assessment, a department of the University of Cambridge.

We share the University's mission to contribute to society through the pursuit of education, learning and research at the highest international levels of excellence.

www.cambridge.org
Information on this title: www.cambridge.org/9781316518212

DOI: 10.1017/9781108999687

First published 2023

A catalogue record for this publication is available from the British Library

A Cataloging-in-Publication data record for this book is available from the Library of Congress

ISBN 978-1-316-51821-2 Hardback
ISBN 978-1-108-99574-0 Paperback

Cambridge University Press & Assessment has no responsibility for the persistence or accuracy of URLs for external or third-party internet websites referred to in this publication and does not guarantee that any content on such websites is, or will remain, accurate or appropriate.

The expectation that we can be immersed in suffering and loss daily and not be touched by it is as unrealistic as expecting to walk through water without getting wet.

– Rachel Naomi Remen, M.D.

Contents

Figures

Foreword

In the National Gallery in London, there is a painting – later split into four parts – that depicts the killing of an emperor on June 19, 1867. *The Execution of Maximilian* was put to canvas by the impressionist painter Édouard Manet on three different occasions between 1867 and 1869. The painting was updated as additional news and details arrived in Europe of the death by firing squad of the man that Emperor Napoleon III had initially installed in Mexico, but had now turned against.

This image has always fascinated me, wandering through that gallery on Trafalgar Square. Cut into pieces, we no longer see Maximilian's death (that part has been lost), but we know the guns have been fired by his six uniformed executioners (a seventh stands behind, ready to deliver a final shot if needed). It was the invisibility of Maximilian's death that fascinated me. It caused me to pause beside the canvas and picture in my head Maximilian's last moments, to ask myself how he looked, to wonder what he must have been thinking. Manet's depiction of this scene was a political act: As an ardent republican, the artist created the graphic image to oppose the policies of Napoleon III. The execution had caused shockwaves in Paris as society asked why France had failed to support or save the very emperor it had installed (Figure o.1).

Indeed, the painting is intended to shock. Of course, this was neither the first nor the last time that graphic imagery had been used for political ends. But today, as this painting sits alongside works of Cézanne, Degas, and Pissarro, with visitors to the gallery wandering past and admiring its composition, I doubt, when the finest details of conflicts and natural disasters can be viewed immediately on a screen held in the palm of their hands, they are as struck by the painting's graphic nature as a viewer would have been in the 1860s.

Depictions of conflict, violence, and human suffering have been with us throughout history – to oppose, to celebrate, or to simply report global events. Shortly before Maximilian's execution, Alexander Gardner and James Gibson, working with Mathew Brady to document the US Civil War of 1861 to 1865, photographed dead soldiers on the battlefield of Antietam. Zainul Abedin sketched and painted the victims of the 1943 Bengal famine. Malangatana Ngwenya's arrest in 1964 for aiding independence movements in Mozambique led to his graphic, grotesque drawings

FIGURE 0.1 The Execution of Emperor Maximilian (1867–69), oil on canvas.
Source: National Gallery, London

of torture at the hands of the Portuguese secret police. Margaret Bourke-White's images of the liberation of concentration camps in 1945, Sebastião Salgado's photographs of the conditions of workers in Brazilian gold mines, or Fernando Botero's series of drawings and paintings depicting the torture of Iraqi prisoners by their American captors at Abu Ghraib prison in Baghdad: Arresting images can change how we see the world. To quote the artist Joan Miró: "You can look at a picture for a week and never think of it again. You can also look at a picture for a second and think of it all your life." Pictures such as these – created to document human cruelty and injustice, or to inspire political or social change – are the ones that we look at for a second and think of all our life. Therein lies their power.

When I started working with graphic imagery in the early 2000s, my team and I were gatekeepers. Based in a peaceful, major European city, our newsroom would decide what images to share with broadcasters, who would decide, in turn, what their viewers would see. Our choices were driven by what we editorially judged would make headline news across the European continent. I covered all of what would be described as the major news stories of the first decade of the new century: the 2003 invasion of Iraq and its subsequent insurgency, the civil war in Liberia that finished the same year, the tsunami in the Indian Ocean in 2004, the 2010 earthquake in Haiti, and terrorist attacks on public transport in Madrid in 2004 and London in 2007. I remember seeing the first bombs fall on Baghdad, the mangled wreck of an exploded bus in central London, and the bodies of gassed and executed militants and their hostages in a Moscow theater. These were images that were hard to look at, that I will think of all my life. For the most part, these images were captured by professionals, camera people, or photographers trained to understand what could be shown to the public – and whose training told them what not to film, what not to share, and how to use an image to tell a story without depicting the full horror of what had happened. It was a world where much of a story could be told through a viewer's imagination.

There were, of course, also instances when the full horror was depicted. On the first of September 2004, over 1,100 people were taken hostage in a school in the town of Beslan, in the Russian republic of North Ossetia. Three days later, the siege was lifted by Russian security forces at the cost of 333 lives – 186 of them children. The operation to lift the siege was broadcast live to the world through the cameras of the global news organizations that were gathered outside. The nature of the imagery shown that day led the same organizations to later introduce time delays of several seconds to their live coverage of sensitive events to avoid sending out the most sickening imagery to their audiences. Working in a newsroom on that story remains one of my most upsetting professional experiences. I spent several days rerunning the pictures of the school children fleeing a place that should have been safe for them through my head, wondering how I would have reacted in the same situation, wondering how they must have been feeling having survived when many of their classmates had not. Several years later, when conducting my own research into the impact of distressing imagery, an interviewee suggested that there were "three-pint and five-pint videos," referencing how much beer you would need to drink after viewing them. Those words took me straight back to Beslan and that newsroom where any discussion of the impact on yourself of working on such upsetting events was taboo. But for the public, this was still an isolated event even though some lurid shots got through, broadcast by media gatekeepers to the world.

The role of newsroom gatekeepers was already changing when anti-government protests overtook Tunisia in 2010. By then, Facebook and YouTube had already existed for over half a decade, Twitter for slightly less. The uprisings across Tunisia and, subsequently, Egypt, Bahrain, Yemen, Libya, and Syria changed newsgathering and reporting forever. Anyone could now tell their stories of the suffering they had witnessed or experienced, and they did. Protesters organized on Facebook and shared videos of protests on YouTube – and all thanks to the mobile telephones carrying cheap image sensors in their hands. This shift toward "citizen journalism" was particularly marked in these countries, where state news organizations had been telling their rulers' stories to the world, and nobody else's. As civil conflicts broke out and the countries involved became more hazardous, journalists, human rights researchers, and humanitarian workers unable to access affected regions could turn to social media to find evidence of massacres in Cairo, airstrikes in Benghazi, or executions in Raqqa. Reporting and research could be supplemented with "user-generated content" as it was then called, or "open-source information" as it is often called now.

The biggest change in this new era of newsgathering was the volume of unmediated content. The large numbers of people now owning mobile telephones with cameras and high-speed mobile Internet connections meant that there was no longer one professionally filmed video of an event, but twenty videos shot by bystanders.

The descriptions that accompanied these quick-circulating videos weren't always accurate, and sometimes dangerously misleading, especially the further they sped from the original source. After a period of repeatedly broadcasting misattributed videos, making mistake upon mistake, it became apparent that newsrooms wanting to use these videos needed to verify them rigorously. Just as Édouard Manet had to piece together the facts of Maximilian's death from small details garnered from disparate reports and accounts, the verifiers of videos, journalists, or human rights researchers sitting far away from the violence in their offices in Doha, Beirut, or Nairobi, had to learn how to validate the authenticity of the videos and photographs posted to social media. This meant interrogating the content for the smallest details, often reviewing the graphic aftermath of distressing events on a loop. The risk of vicarious trauma due to being exposed to distressing experiences even when not physically present became an issue. Or, rather, vicarious trauma finally became *recognized* as an issue not only for those who scrutinized distressing imagery as part of their work, including journalists, human rights researchers, and humanitarian workers, but also for content moderators employed by the social media companies to keep that very nasty content off their platforms.

The fifth edition of the *Diagnostic and Statistical Manual of Mental Disorders*, published in 2013 by the American Psychiatric Association to help professionals diagnose mental disorders in their patients, notes that viewing graphic videos can lead to post-traumatic stress disorder or similar symptoms *if* that viewing is linked to a professional occupation. As I conducted my own research into vicarious trauma and started training news and human rights organizations on mitigating its impact, a common question I encountered was why the diagnosis was specifically linked to occupation. Could not every viewer of graphic imagery be potentially impacted by trauma, especially since anyone can find just about anything now through a quick online search, such as live streams from post-coup protests in Myanmar or videos on Telegram of casualties from the conflict in Ukraine? While I am not a psychiatrist and unable to answer the query, the question of the possible psychological and social impacts of graphic content, regardless of whether it deserves a specific psychiatric label in the general population, seems particularly important to address. Just this question is one reason this book is so important, so welcome, and so needed. Our world is now saturated with graphic imagery, streaming from every one of its corners, and we are all potentially at risk.

Édouard Manet had to wait two years to obtain the details of an execution by firing squad on a different continent. Today, we may wait less than two seconds for upsetting images to arrive, often without warning. We must understand the impact that has on each of us in our society and how we can minimize serious negative effects yet still acknowledge the wrongs of the world and find ways to address them as we navigate the seas of graphic imagery.

Sam Dubberley
Human Rights Watch, Berlin
2022

Acknowledgments

Every author owes a debt of gratitude to the people who surround them – who give form to their thoughts, who feed their souls, and who help shape their personal and professional lives. We are so grateful to the community of people who have continually encouraged us and convinced us of the need for this book.

Our initial thanks go to Elizabeth Farnsworth and Sam Dubberley. When we first clasped hands and took our terrifying leap into founding the Human Rights Center Investigations Lab, it was they who gave us the nudge we needed, but also helped us understand how psychologically perilous this journey would be. It was they who shone a light on where we'd need to go in order to gather support for our students. They warned us that our focus on resilience would have to be laser-sharp. It's because they pointed us in the right direction years ago that we've been able to follow in the footsteps of the brilliant pioneers who forged a path before us, instead of stumbling and getting tangled in the brambles, while heading to new insights.

A huge thank you to Matt Gallaway for taking a chance on our ideas for this book and being such a thoughtful and insightful editor, pushing us to make this book broader and deeper. We are grateful to you and to everyone at Cambridge University Press who has played a role in bringing *Graphic* into being and launching it into the world, so that it can be a resource for those who are working on how to make engagement with social media as healthy, as meaningful, and as rewarding as possible.

Thank you also to Deborah and Stephen Goldblatt for opening their home to us and providing an art-filled haven in which to write for a few precious days in July 2019, days that helped us focus and finally start this book. You have been so generous, not only introducing us to new ideas and new communities but also to people whose thoughts on resilience in the face of the unanticipated twists and turns of life can only be described as profound. San Miguel de Allende will always live in the heart of this project.

Thanks to Mesa Refuge in Pt. Reyes. Peter and Susan, the house you've filled with so many creative spirits and books on the wild edge of the California coast was the leaping-off point for this project, as it has been for so many others. Stepping into the closet of each bedroom and reverently running our eyes and fingers along the signatures of the authors who came before us – authors who left us awe-filled – dared us to think this might be possible. What a gift!

Thank you to Pittsburgh artists Max Gonzales, Shane Pilster, Jerome Charles, and Brian Gonnella, who generously recounted the creation story of the Black Lives Matter waterfront murals, depicted in a photograph originally chosen for the cover of *Graphic*, for their openness, insights, and transformational practices in art and life.

Thank you also to Jonathan Cobb, whose comments, edits, questions, and suggested edits improved this book immensely. Taleen Sample and Olivia Wendel: You repeatedly stunned us with the quality of research and the original insights you shared during that COVID summer you worked with us, which included topics as diverse as PTSI, PTSD, identity, trolling, and the gamification of online spaces. It was shocking to realize that you were only high school students (impossible). You are going to help lead the world someday and we're relieved to know it. Thanks also to Sydney Saubestre, Shakiba Mashayekhi, Diana Chavez-Varela, and Kate Pundyk for helping to get us through the finish line: Your research support and your emotional support have been invaluable. We are grateful to call you colleagues and friends.

To the UC Berkeley Student Technology Fund, the University of California Multicampus Research Projects and Initiatives Fund, the Public Interest Technology University Network, the Oak Foundation, Open Society Foundations, and Sigrid Rausing Trust: Thank you for taking a chance on our work at the intersection of technology and human rights, which helped generate many of the concepts in this book. To Tom White: Thank you for sponsoring our time at Mesa Refuge, along with so generously sponsoring the Human Rights Center fellows who shared the house with us and gave us critical feedback on our proposal. To Sylvanna Falcon and Saskia Nauenberg Dunkall of UCSC's Investigations Lab; Jessica Peake of UCLA's Investigations Lab; Stephanie Croft, Sofia-Lissett Kooner, Gisela Perez de Acha, and Brian Nguyen of the Human Rights Center Investigations Lab; Maggie Andresen, Eric Stover, Betsy Popken, Lindsay Freeman, Alan Iijima, Ana Linares Montoya and Alexey Berlind of the Human Rights Center; Nicki Lewis, Nisha Srinivasa, Mazelle Etessami, Jon Ortilla, Youstina Youssef, Nilsu Celikel, Than Mai Bercher, Stefanie Le, Dohee Kim, and Sonnet Phelps who worked on community and resiliency in the Investigations Lab or at the Human Rights Center; and all of the leaders of the Digital Verification Corps: Thank you for helping to build the collegial, collaborative world of digital investigations that we're so grateful to be part of.

Finally, thank you to all of the students who have ever been a part of the Human Rights Center Investigations Lab and to everyone who agreed to be interviewed for or has otherwise fed this book. Your bravery, generosity, vulnerability, and thoughtfulness have offered everything of worth that's included here. We only hope we have done your insights and your stories justice. You have been pioneers in a sometimes exciting but also difficult and thorny new world and have laid a critical piece of the foundation upon which our new digital-physical universe is being built. It is because of your fierce insistence that we pay attention to issues of resiliency during that process that we retain our hope for the future and dare to dream that the world we collectively create can be beautiful.

From Alexa: My son was born in 2004, the year that Facebook made its debut; my daughter in 2007, the year the iPhone launched. Their lives have been inevitably shaped by social media and the content that comes with it. That exposure has made them far more globally aware than I was as a teenager, and so much more digitally savvy. But it also means that they've been far more exposed to graphic and potentially damaging online material and have had to grapple with a new layer to social life that earlier generations never had to. And it means that as a parent I'm in much the same boat as others: struggling to figure out how to keep our children relatively safe online and offline, empowering them to make healthy choices, while engaging with the reality that we are (as a colleague of ours frequently points out) not only physical beings but also digital ones (thank you Gisela!), whose on- and offline identities are inextricably intertwined. Thank you Zander and Sophie for helping me understand the layers to this that I never could on my own. You know the boundaries of our digital world better than I ever will and I am so grateful for all that you've taught me. Don, you have given me a life for which I'm so thankful; I could never do this work without you stepping up and stepping forward to cover everything that falls to the wayside when I fall down a rabbit hole, and I know it. Thank you also for your keen honesty when reading what I write. That brutal but loving feedback builds a trust and a security that allows me to get ever closer to saying something honest. Wendy, the fact that my mother is a psychotherapist with a (major) crush on the brain, who has spent most of her career thinking about our reactions to trauma, who sparkles with excitement every time those conversations come up and go deep, is imprinted on everything I do, like an accent that betrays my origins. My final solo thanks, however, must go to Andrea. I can't imagine a better writing and thinking partner, the almost instinctive push-pull, stepping forward and stepping back, that have made this such a meaningful dance. Thank you for pulling me out of my own dissociation and reminding me how important it is to feel. Thank you for being my professional co-parent and co-pilot. I'm so proud of the territories we've traveled and the work babies we've birthed!

From Andrea: My father often had a book in his hands or a newspaper on his lap. I wish more than anything he were here to read this book. I'm grateful for my beautiful mom, Stella, who always makes me laugh, and loving step-dad, Patrick; my best friends (who happen to be my siblings) Marcus and Georgia; Bobbi for the confidence and curiosity you instilled; and for each and every member of my brilliant Fike family. Every day, I give thanks to my partner, John, and kids, Angie, Melina, and Devin, for what you give to the world and how you teach me to be present, joyful, engaged, and optimistic. Through the pandemic, we shared time-bending days scattered throughout the house in Zoom classes, calls, and interviews, writing, or playing with our beloved puppy, Louie. I will never forgot or take for granted this found time. Alexa has been the best writing partner, colleague, mentor, and friend on this project and over the past ten years of our work together. I have loved and will miss germinating this project with you during our 10 am Friday meetings, and only hope that we may do so again and again. How is it possible to work so closely with someone and rarely if ever feel frustration or angst and to feel more respect and appreciation each day? Such is the case. Thanks also to Eric Stover, our faculty director at the Human Rights Center, who is my ethical and literary guiding star, teacher, and friend. As we have noted, the students we work with at UC Berkeley and around the world are the heart and soul of this place. They have taken up the sorely needed work of documenting human rights violations through digital investigations and taken to heart the need for resiliency practices in our work and life. Our students have informed and enabled this book. Finally, I want to appreciate the human rights workers, journalists, and others on the frontlines around the world who inspire this book. We write it because we want people to go toward humanity and not run away, to grapple with the pain and not shrink from it, and to be fully and healthfully in the struggle for a better world right now and for as long as it takes.

Interviewees

- **Adam Brown:** Associate Professor of Psychology (Clinical) and Vice Provost for Research at the New School and Director of the Trauma and Global Mental Health Lab. He is a member of the Human Rights Resilience Project, "an interdisciplinary group of scholars and practitioners carrying out research and creating tools to improve resiliency and well-being in the human rights community."
- **Adebayo Okeowo:** Africa Program Manager for the nonprofit organization WITNESS, which provides resources and training to help people create user-generated content to hold power to account. A human rights lawyer with more than a decade of experience working on issues of socioeconomic rights, environmental justice, and international criminal accountability. Former Lab Manager for the University of Pretoria hub of Amnesty International's Digital Verification Corps.
- **AnaStacia Nicol Wright:** Staff attorney at Worksafe, a California-based nonprofit organization that promotes and protects the right of all people to have a safe and healthy workplace. Former content moderator.
- **Ariel Newman:** A nineteen-year-old freshman at Sonoma State University (at the time of her interview), who grew up in Berkeley.
- **Ashley Bradford:** Senior Vice President for Learning Technology at 2U. Former CEO of CritiqueIt, Inc., a technology company that develops tools for annotating text, audio, and video documents. Worked with a team of UC Berkeley students to create a tool for giving online investigators greater control over their exposure to graphic and other upsetting online content.
- **Brandie Nonnecke:** Ph.D., Founding Director of the Center for Information Technology Research in the Interest of Society (CITRIS) Policy Lab at UC Berkeley; Technology and Human Rights Fellow at the Carr Center for Human Rights Policy at the Harvard Kennedy School; and Fellow at the Schmidt Futures International Strategy Forum.
- **Christoph Koettl [multiple interviews]:** Visual investigations journalist with the *New York Times*, who specializes in geospatial and open-source research and lends expertise on armed conflicts and human rights violations. Former senior analyst at Amnesty International.

- **Eileen Clancy [multiple interviews]:** Archivist and expert in the history of science and computing with a focus on how knowledge is created and represented. Pioneered strategies for holding power to account with user-generated content; co-founder of I-Witness Video.
- **Elena Martin[1]:** Former student team member at the Human Rights Center Investigations Lab.
- **Elizabeth (Liz) Scott[2]:** Software engineer who has worked for a number of tech companies. Former global policy operations manager for YouTube, who has supervised content moderation teams.
- **Emiliana Simon-Thomas:** Science Director of the Greater Good Science Center, including co-instructor of the center's *Science of Happiness* and *Science of Happiness at Work* online courses. Leading expert on the neuroscience and psychology of compassion, kindness, gratitude, and other prosocial skills. Researcher into how unpleasant emotions influence thinking and decision-making. Occasional advisor to social media tech companies.
- **Frank Ochberg [multiple interviews]:** Psychiatrist and pioneer in trauma science. Wrote the first text on how to treat post-traumatic stress disorder, which he has retitled "post-traumatic stress injury." Clinical professor of psychiatry at Michigan State University, chairman emeritus of the Dart Center for Journalism and Trauma, and founder of the organizations Gift From Within and Critical Incident Analysis Group.
- **Gabriela (Gabi) Ivens:** Head of open-source research and member of the Digital Investigations Lab at Human Rights Watch, where she conducts online investigations into human rights violations and other atrocities, works to build internal capacity, and sets up robust and ethical processes for conducting open-source investigations. Currently on the board of Mnemonic, a human rights organization in Berlin, Ivens is a former Ford-Mozilla fellow at WITNESS and led the investigative portal *Exposing the Invisible* at the nonprofit, nongovernmental organization Tactical Technology Collective.
- **Haley Willis [multiple interviews]:** Visual investigations reporter at the *New York Times* and former student team lead and trainer for the Human Rights Center Investigations Lab.
- **Josiah "Tink" Thompson:** Former private investigator and former philosophy professor who has used user-generated content to (most famously) investigate the killing of President John F. Kennedy. Thompson has advanced the theory that more than one shooter took part in President Kennedy's murder. Author of *Six Seconds in Dallas* and *Last Second in Dallas*, which detail his investigation.
- **Keramet Reiter:** Professor and Vice Chair of Criminology, Law and Society at UC Irvine's School of Law. Director of *LIFTED*, which provides educational

---

[1] This is a pseudonym.
[2] This is a pseudonym.

opportunities for prisoners and former prisoners, and co-founder of *PrisonPandemic*, which maps the spread of COVID among California's prison population. An expert in prisons, prisoners' rights, solitary confinement, and the impact of prison and punishment policy on individuals, communities, and legal systems. Author of *23/7: Pelican Bay Prison and the Rise of Long-Term Solitary Confinement.*

- **Laura van Dernoot Lipsky:** Founder and Director of The Trauma Stewardship Institute and author of the bestselling book *Trauma Stewardship: An Everyday Guide to Caring for Self While Caring for Others* and *Age of Overwhelm*. An expert on trauma exposure who started her over thirty-five-year career working in a homeless shelter, and eventually working with survivors of child abuse, domestic violence, sexual assault, natural disasters, and other forms of trauma. Lipsky spoke to students in our Investigations Lab in fall 2019.

- **Mallika Kaur:** Lecturer at Berkeley Law, as well as a lawyer and writer who has worked with victim-survivors of gendered violence for more than two decades, including as an emergency room crisis counselor and as an expert witness on intimate partner violence and sexual violence. Author of *Faith, Gender, and Activism in the Punjab Conflict: The Wheat Fields Still Whisper.*

- **Mariana Jones**[3]: Former trust and safety officer at two major social media companies who regularly conducted online investigations based on user-generated content.

- **Meg Satterthwaite:** Professor of Clinical Law and Faculty Director of the Center for Human Rights and Global Justice and of the Robert and Helen Bernstein Institute for Human Rights at New York University School of Law. Director of NYU's Global Justice Clinic. Expert on legal empowerment, vicarious trauma, and well-being among human rights workers. Co-lead of the Human Rights Resilience Project, which documents, raises awareness, and develops culturally sensitive training programs to promote well-being and resilience among human rights workers. Appointed as United Nations Special Rapporteur on the independence of judges and lawyers by the Human Rights Council in October 2022.

- **Michael Elsanadi:** Investigator at the Syrian Archive, trainer in open-source investigations at UC Berkeley's Human Rights Center and School of Journalism, and former student team lead at the Human Rights Center Investigations Lab.

- **Michael Shaw [multiple interviews]:** Psychologist with expertise in responses to visual imagery and both professional and personal well-being. Longtime advisor to businesses and academic institutions. Analyst of and frequent lecturer about news photos and visual journalism, as well as co-founder of the nonprofit organization ReadingThePictures.org, which provides daily analysis and commentary of news images and visual politics and promotes visual and media literacy. The online discussion series, ReadingThePictures Salon, analyzes how media frame major social issues and key news events.

---

[3] This is a pseudonym.

- **Open Source Researchers of Color Collective:** OSROC was created by six UC Berkeley graduates to provide resources on and strengthen digital literacy, privacy/security, and ethical investigations of human rights violations for diverse audiences.
- **Rachael Cornejo:** Operational cybersecurity expert and former student team lead for the Human Rights Center Investigations Lab. Co-founder of RatedR and Open Source Researchers of Color Collective.
- **Ronald Dahl:** Professor of Community Health Sciences for UC Berkeley's Joint Medical Program, Director of the Institute of Human Development, and Founding Director of the Center for the Developing Adolescent. A pediatrician and developmental scientist with long-standing research interests in affect regulation and the development of behavioral and emotional disorders in children and adolescents.
- **Sam Dubberley:** Managing Director of Human Rights Watch's Digital Investigations Lab, former head of Amnesty International's Evidence Lab and manager of the Crisis Response Team's Digital Verification Corps, an international consortium of university centers and students that conduct online human rights investigations in support of Amnesty International's research. Former journalist and fellow of the Tow Center for Digital Journalism at Columbia University. Co-editor of the book *Digital Witness: Using Open Source Information for Human Rights Investigation, Documentation and Accountability*.
- **Wendy Kirk:** Ph.D., psychotherapist, and marriage, family and child counselor who conducted her dissertation on survivor guilt in women who have elective abortions and has long worked with people experiencing trauma and secondary trauma. Kirk is related to the book's author, Alexa Koenig.
- **Whitney Hurst:** Senior producer for the *New York Times* visual investigations team. Her work includes the *New York Times* seminal analysis of the killing of George Floyd.
- **William Mansson:** A twenty-two-year-old (at the time of his interview) who grew up in Sweden and attended Penn State University.

Introduction

Taking in Trauma from Our Newsfeed

Bodies wrapped in black plastic bags are thrown into a makeshift mass grave by stunned and stone-faced men, landing with thuds, each upon another.

A man enters a hospital carrying a baby in a blood-stained blanket, one tiny limp hand poking out. A distraught mother follows just behind (see Figure I.1).

A woman plays her piano in a bombed out home, a note of elegance amid the destruction around her.

A person riding their bike on a lonely suburban street turns a corner, dismounts, and is suddenly felled as armored vehicles fire multiple rounds.

Today, these graphic images are coming from Russia's war in Ukraine, in TikToks and Tweets, on Telegram and the front page of the *Times*, and in our cable and network news broadcasts. On other days, they come from the gun war playing out in America's schools, grocery stores, and churches, or from hundreds of other tragedies around the world. Some are shot by war photographers. Others are captured by victims or soldiers or bystanders. Some are bloody and graphic; others are intimate and haunting; still others are strangely moving in the unexpected normalcy and fearlessness they portray. What images will come tomorrow to those of us not in the crossfire? What images are dinging on our phones, in the middle of dinner, at a bar, at the gym, at our job, or even as you are reading these words?

Even those who deal with graphic images professionally are struggling to adapt to just how inundated we've all become with such imagery and how it can pop up in the most banal of contexts. A journalist explained what the onslaught of graphic imagery sometimes feels like for him: "Scrolling through my Twitter feed today I saw a pretty gruesome image of a bloody baby, apparently from Ukraine. I immediately looked away, but I'm sure I will see many more images in the coming days and weeks that I don't necessarily want to see. ... It's just showing up on my scroll. I've got the latest news from spring

FIGURE I.1 Marina Yatsko, left, runs behind her boyfriend Fedor who carries her recently killed eighteen-month-old son Kirill into a hospital in Mariupol, Ukraine, on Friday, March 4, 2022.
Source: AP Photo/Evgeniy Maloletka

training with the Mets and then the next image is something I can't get out of my head.[1]"

Some of the most horrifying and provocative images of recent years have come not just from war zones, however, but from the streets of the United States, such as graphic imagery of the murder of George Floyd by police in Minneapolis on May 25, 2020. The morning after Floyd's killing, *New York Times* reporter Haley Willis, a member of the paper's Visual Investigations team, was housebound by the COVID-19 pandemic and working in her cramped and unbearably humid bedroom in Brooklyn, poring over the amateur videos that had captured his killing.

Willis had already viewed some of the viral videos on her social media feed of Minneapolis Police Officer Derek Chauvin with his knee planted on George Floyd's neck (see Figure I.2), but she had not really *seen* the footage with her reporter's eye. She played the first shaky video all the way through, taking in details that were obvious or subtle, relevant, and not relevant:

Police officers approach a blue SUV, a passenger door is ajar, transit buses pass, an officer pulls a gun, a Black man is face down on the pavement, the man pleads, "Mama" and "I can't breathe."

Willis watched these images alone, far from the bustling pre-pandemic *New York Times* newsroom on Manhattan's 8th Avenue and miles from her fellow reporters, including Senior Producer Whitney Hurst in Brooklyn, and senior editors upstate in their "pandemic" homes. Although the apartment she shared with an acquaintance was moldy and graced by an occasional cockroach, Willis's room was tidy and her desk even tidier, much like her desk at the *Times*, which was so sparse that

---

[1] Matt Katz, 'We Were Warned: War Crimes Tribunals in the Digital Age,' *On The Media*, March 18, 2022 (discussed from 11:00 on).

FIGURE I.2 Minneapolis Police Officer Derek Chauvin fatally kneeling on the neck of George Floyd.
Source: Frame taken from video by Darnella Frazier

colleagues had initially wondered, half-jokingly, if she might be a spy. From her bedroom/home office, she watched the footage frame by frame a second time, and then a third, and fourth. She paused to grab a cup of green tea and a breath. Willis clicked "play" again, this time with the sound down because Floyd's cries had gotten under her skin.

The Visual Investigations team at the *New York Times* has pioneered methods of analyzing digital material, such as videos and photos, and creating visual timelines to illuminate facts and tell stories. Willis, a relatively new member of the team at that time, was charged with reviewing all of the available videos of George Floyd's murder to see if the team could tell a fuller story than what the public already knew of what had happened in Floyd's final minutes. She watched footage from security cameras, time stamped incorrectly; a shaky video taken by a bystander who was told to step away; and the now-infamous video of the moments before, during, and after George Floyd's murder by Minneapolis police officers, captured by teenager Darnela Frazier.

Although just twenty-two years old at the time, Willis was already a seasoned viewer of horrific videos. Years before, she had joined the Human Rights Center Investigations Lab as a nineteen-year-old Sociology and Media Studies major from outside of Austin, Texas. During her three years in the Lab, she was at the vanguard of a burgeoning field of online open-source investigations, which uses social media and other information on the Internet to investigate human rights violations and international crimes. Faculty, staff, and more experienced students in the Human Rights Center's Lab trained incoming students to conduct this work for organizations doing research, journalism, and law. A leader on the team, Willis often analyzed videos for Amnesty International and the Syrian Archive. She had pored over distressing footage of police beating protesters and blasting communities with tear gas, brutal detentions, and murders perpetrated in broad daylight – events that spanned the globe from Mozambique to Myanmar.

Now she was taking in every detail of a man's last minutes in Minneapolis: the eerie quiet of this violence, punctuated by the intermittent and increasingly panicked cries of bystanders. "My colleague Christiaan [Triebert] and I viewed it multiple times – maybe a dozen times – just to count how many times George Floyd says, 'I can't breathe,'" said Willis, explaining a step in the painstaking process she used to analyze the videos of his death.

Floyd cried out, Willis and Triebert found, at least sixteen times in less than five minutes before falling silent. The amateur video captured Floyd's eyes closing, a male bystander shouting, "Bro, he's not fucking moving," and Chauvin shoving his knee deeper into Floyd's neck.

"When the officer says he can't find a pulse, it's like a stab to the heart. They knew they were killing somebody," said Willis, her voice rising as she scrolled through the images again in her mind.

The resulting *New York Times* video – "8 Minutes and 46 Seconds: How George Floyd was Killed in Police Custody"[2] – along with the underlying videos filmed and uploaded by people who were present, was viewed by 87 percent of Black Americans and 79 percent of all people in the United States, according to a Washington Post/Ipsos poll.[3] With screen time up nationwide due to COVID quarantining and nearly doubling among adolescents,[4] as reported by a Los Angeles copyright monitoring firm, a captive global audience would view George Floyd's murder and related Black Lives Matter videos an estimated 1.4 billion times in the ten days after his killing.[5]

George Floyd's murder – recorded by ordinary citizens and posted online as user-generated content – was far from the first horrific, graphic incident to be captured on camera and shared for public viewing via mainstream media, however. There was,

[2] Evan Hill, Ainara Tiefenthäler, Christiaan Triebert, Drew Jordan, Haley Willis, and Robin Stein, "8 Minutes and 46 Seconds: How George Floyd Was Killed in Police Custody," *New York Times*, May 31, 2020.

[3] Washington Post/Ipsos poll, conducted June 9–14, 2020, random national sample, available at: www.washingtonpost.com/context/june-9-14-2020-washington-post-ipsos-poll/9da7d577-8bba-4319-97bb-2cea5aebca7e/.

[4] B. E. Wagner, A. L. Folk, S. L. Hahn, D. J. Barr-Anderson, N. Larson, and D. Neumark-Sztainer, "Recreational Screen Time Behaviors during the COVID-19 Pandemic in the U.S.: A Mixed-Methods Study among a Diverse Population-Based Sample of Emerging Adults," 18(9) *International Journal of Environmental Research and Public Health* 4613 (2021). https://doi.org/10.3390/ije

[5] Sam Blake, "George Floyd Protest Videos Were Watched over 1.4 Billion Times in I First 12 Days of Unrest," Dot.LA, June 12, 2020 (citing an L.A.-based analytics and digital rights management firm).

for example, the image of Emmett Till's mutilated and bloated body in his casket: "I wanted the world to see what they did to my baby," said Mamie Till, Emmett's mother, about her son who was beaten, shot, and drowned in the Mississippi Delta in 1955;[6] the shooting of President John F. Kennedy, taken by amateur photographer Abraham Zapruder, the president's head blown open beside his wife in a motorcade convertible in 1963; footage of Rodney King being pulled from a car to be beaten and kicked by Los Angeles police officers, recorded by George Holliday on a Sony Handycam video camera in 1991; and videos of children unable to breathe after a chemical weapons attack in Douma, Syria, captured and uploaded by aid workers in 2018.

None of us are strangers to this content. In today's information age, we can watch graphic events daily, like the livestream of a mass shooting in Christchurch, New Zealand, or a video of a Burmese soldier shooting a man in broad daylight. We can watch live pornography, even of children, even if illegal. And it's not just overt human-on-human violence: We might stumble upon the video of a Florida apartment complex swallowing up ninety-eight people in a matter of seconds; stampeding fires, tsunamis, and earthquakes – all images that can be as disturbing as any captured in a war zone. What was once a rare glimpse into the world's horrors, if you weren't living one of them yourself, is now commonplace on our handheld screens.

Since the dawn of Facebook in 2004, YouTube in 2005, Twitter in 2006, the iPhone in 2007, and the global proliferation of smartphones and social media platforms that followed, the creation and spread of what's called user-generated content or open-source information has skyrocketed, for good and bad. Videos of mass killings and other horrific events now come to us, sometimes in real time, via live streaming and other digital processes that are vivid and immediate, dissipating the difference between witnessing such horrible events in person and witnessing them on a screen.

This open-source content is intimate by nature: a video shot in the midst of a human rights violation may not only show us blood and death but may expose us to expressions of a person's terror in the moment, their breathy commentary and anguished cries. Some of these raw videos can bring us into the experience in a direct and painful way – more so than an edited and packaged newscast. We are put in the shoes of an often-relatable viewer who is recording the violence in real time, while expressing fear or grief or anger. This content is often shared not only for the narrative it advances (as with professional footage) but also for shock value in order to inspire action (i.e., clicks) and thus may be especially provocative or graphic, unlike the carefully curated images of the past. When atrocities are witnessed by dozens or even hundreds of people, the quantity of videos and photos generated by bystanders can be far greater than the lone professional photo that accompanies a news story.

[6] "When One Mother Defied America: The Photo That Changed the Civil Rights Movement," *Time*, July 10, 2016. As quoted in Time Magazine: "When Till's mother Mamie came to identify her son, she told the funeral director, 'Let the people see what I've seen.'" She kept 14-year-old Emmett's casket open; he was viewed by more than 50,000 people. *Jet*, a Black weekly magazine, ran a photo of Emmett in his casket that was later picked up by other media.

And more change is coming: Even as we chronicle this moment in our information environment, artificial intelligence is further shifting the sands, creating new relationships between us and our exposure to online depictions of violence – both by enabling new ways to create images of violence and affecting how and when we're exposed to it.

Of course, graphic imagery isn't always just gratuitous. Such images have a rich history of being used to inspire action. "For a long time some people believed that if the horror could be made vivid enough, most people would finally take in the outrageousness, the insanity of war"[7] and do whatever they could to stop it, writes Susan Sontag in her seminal book *Regarding the Pain of Others*. She highlights as an example the book *Krieg dem Kriege!* (War against War) by the conscientious objector Ernst Freidrich, who published the book in 1924 as a form of "shock therapy." The book is composed of 180 graphic photos, including 24 close ups of soldiers from World War I with facial wounds. That book, Sontag chronicles, was followed by Virginia Woolf's 1938 anti-war essay *Three Guineas*, drafted as a response to an inquiry about how to prevent war, and filmmaker Abel Gance's 1938 remake of *J'accuse*, which featured close-ups of disfigured combatants: "Fill your eyes with this horror! It is the only thing that can stop you," says the film's protagonist.[8] Sontag also notes that despite these attempts to use graphic images to underscore the importance of peace, World War II started the next year.

What effect does the proliferation of online graphic content have on us individually and as a society? How does our identity – racial or as survivors of violence, for example – impact how this material affects us? Should we develop strategies for taking in this traumatic material or is it better to look away? When should we prioritize one strategy over the other? When do graphic accounts of assaults, such as that on George Floyd, serve as catalysts to protest injustice? When does the volume of violence and trauma become so overwhelming that it dampens our ability to feel the world's pain and hinders our ability to act?

* * *

In *Graphic*, we draw upon the experiences of those who work closely with user-generated content to help answer these and other questions and make sense of this moment. We started our research by noting the experiences of our students and alumni, such as Willis. We also talked with reporters at major news outlets and researchers who have looked closely at the effects of disturbing online content on human rights workers and journalists. We learned from people who have led teams at major social media platforms, as well as the "content moderators" who are often outsourced by major social media platforms and watch thousands of hours of

---

[7] Susan Sontag, *Regarding the Pain of Others* (New York: Picador 2003):14.
[8] Ibid. at 16.

disturbing posts, ranging from terrorism to the sexual exploitation of children, in order to determine if those posts should be removed from the Internet. We talked with professionals in a variety of fields – as well as younger individuals who have grown up in the era of social media – to understand both the importance of graphic and distressing content and how constant exposure to it affects all of us.

As academics, as journalists, and as human rights researchers and investigators, we wrote this book because we see the value of people engaging with difficult visual content in order to better understand our world; to challenge structural racism, sexism, classism, and other forms of violence; to combat state-sponsored violence; to illuminate hate speech and hate crimes; and ultimately, to make change.

Most importantly, we wrote this book to probe the question: How do we as individuals, as communities, and as a global society grapple with and stand against the cruelties of the world without becoming numb to those events or engulfed by them – especially when we watch that violence in almost real-time and in intimate, graphic detail? It's a question that goes as far back, at least, to when an artist first rendered or a photographer first captured or a writer first recounted an image of violence or war and held it up for another to take in, to feel, embrace, oppose, or otherwise judge. The speed and scale of our exposure to graphic imagery may be new, but the need to wrestle with these questions of how we use such imagery is not.

Ultimately, the insights in this book come from our collective decade of working directly with graphic social media content, as well as extensive research that we conducted over a period of five years. This includes desk research that spans multiple disciplines (sociology, psychology, neuroscience, computer science, law, and journalism); various small group conversations; ethnographic observations from our work at UC Berkeley and our partnerships with journalists, lawyers, and human rights advocates; and approximately 100 hours of original interviews with diverse individuals who regularly confront graphic online imagery.[9] We have committed to the tenets of *Data Feminism*, which dictate that we pay attention to who we interview, who we cite, and ultimately whose work and insights we amplify, to ensure equitable inclusion of women, people of color, and others whose contributions may be disproportionately overlooked.[10]

In Chapter 1, we build off this research to summarize how videos and photographs shared in traditional media (such as newspapers, magazines, and television) have historically opened the eyes of people across the world to atrocities, enraging and upsetting them, and in particularly acute cases, igniting a response aimed at social change. This first chapter offers a foundation for thinking about how the videos and photographs disseminated across social media today are both similar to and different from what's come before.

---

[9] We have lightly edited some of the interviews for clarity.
[10] Catherine D'Ignazio and Lauren F. Klein, *Data Feminism* (Cambridge, Massachusetts: MIT Press 2020).

In Chapter 2, we discuss what unites all of us in our response to graphic visual imagery, including what happens biologically when we confront disturbing images.

In Chapter 3, we segue from our similarities to our differences: How our unique identities create variations in how and when we are impacted by graphic online material. For example, how do we respond to material differently, based on our age, race, ethnicity, gender, or geography? We also discuss a fundamental strategy for taking in traumatic content safely: building awareness of our reactions to various forms of content and when we start to be affected by it, including what is especially hard for each of us to endure. This awareness includes how we are likely to react based on our identities and experiences but also how others may respond differently than we do.

In Chapter 4, we pivot to what each of us can do to minimize harm and maximize value from our online lives, including what additional protections we can put in place when viewing content to which we might be emotionally susceptible. We offer hands-on tips and tricks aimed at increasing control over our online engagement in ways that are known to protect.

In Chapter 5, we explore the value of community and collective experience, examining the protective force of our friends, colleagues, and loved ones and discussing what we can do to better protect each other. We look at ways to cultivate and call on our communities in order to process and make meaning from the information in our news feeds.

In Chapter 6, we explore how to foster resilience to the potential negative ramifications of upsetting imagery, including by discerning meaning from time spent on the Internet.

In Chapter 7, we move from an individual and community perspective to a global one. We close with a series of policy recommendations for companies and governments to engage them in fostering an operational and legal environment that will better help people stay psychologically safe when engaging with life online.

* * *

So what are the risks from exposure to graphic imagery that we are hoping this book will help people avoid? Most peoples' reactions to viewing violent or harmful acts – even strong, passionate, and overwhelmed reactions – will fall within a vast range of what can be considered normal human responses to upsetting events. Our aim with this book is to share how to spot potential dangers and what to do when you spot them – not to diagnose or pathologize but to create greater self-awareness and facilitate greater meaning from our online engagement.

One of the risks is indirect trauma, which can be further categorized as either vicarious or secondary trauma. The American Psychological Association defines trauma simply as an "emotional response to a terrible event," a definition that is, to say the least, potentially inclusive of a huge swath of reactions.[11] The APA notes that shock and denial are common responses to extreme events and that longer term manifestations of trauma may range from unpredictable emotions to physical symptoms, such as nausea, a racing heartbeat, or sleeplessness.[12] Traumatic experiences often involve all of our senses and become stored in our long-term memory. Once stored, the trauma can be retriggered by something small, even a smell or a sound.[13]

The effects of trauma exposure may be direct – caused by watching a disturbing or emotionally challenging video of events that have happened to others – or may be indirect. Exposure may also stir a reaction derived from a previous trauma we've personally experienced.[14] For example, the witnessing of police brutality against a Black man may connect with the viewer's own experiences of racial violence or mistreatment, triggering a deeper reaction.

The term vicarious trauma refers to the "acute distress" that may emerge after exposure to *another* person's traumatic experience. It is often used to describe a cumulative phenomenon, such as when a therapist starts to be affected by repeat exposure to their patient's suffering. Such exposure may produce a reaction as significant as a shift in worldview.[15] By contrast, secondary traumatic stress reactions (or simply "secondary trauma") can be more immediate, resulting from a single exposure. Secondary traumatic stress has also been described as the manifestation of indirect traumatization – the resulting actions or reactions, such as abuse of alcohol or drugs for "emotional numbing."[16] Sometimes secondary trauma is described as the "emotional residue" that remains when we "become witnesses to the pain, fear and terror that trauma survivors have endured."[17] The terms vicarious trauma and secondary trauma, while technically distinct, are often used interchangeably by laypersons.

Post-traumatic stress disorder (PTSD), also known as post-traumatic stress injury (PTSI), affects people who have experienced or witnessed a traumatic event "or who have been threatened with death, sexual violence or serious injury" and who

---

[11] World Health Organization, "COVID 19 Virtual Press Conference Transcript," March 5, 2021, available at: www.who.int/publications/m/item/covid-19-virtual-press-conference-transcript—5-march-2021. As the COVID-19 pandemic has taken millions of lives around the world and led to unprecedented shifts in how we live, work, and imagine our future, we may be living in a context of "collective trauma" or "mass trauma." General Tedros Adhanom Ghebreyesus, appointed director of the World Health Organization (WHO) in 2017, said at a 2021 news conference about the COVID-19 pandemic: "Almost the whole world is affected, each and every individual on the surface of the world actually has been affected. ... And that means mass trauma, which is beyond proportion, even bigger than what the world experienced after the Second World War." He warned that this mass trauma will affect the mental health of people for generations to come.

[12] American Psychological Association, "Trauma," at www.apa.org/topics/trauma

[13] Interview by the authors with Dr. Wendy Kirk, January 15, 2022.

[14] Ibid.

[15] Ibid.

[16] Ibid.

[17] American Counseling Association, "Fact Sheet #9: Vicarious Trauma," available at: www.counseling .org/docs/trauma-disaster/fact-sheet-9—vicarious-trauma.pdf.

have as a consequence "intense, disturbing thoughts and feelings related to their experience that last long after the traumatic event has ended."[18] What we call PTSD today was once referred to as "shell shock" or "combat fatigue,"[19] but it doesn't only affect people who have experienced trauma in the context of conflict or war. The APA also notes that PTSD can result from indirect forms of trauma: "For example, PTSD could occur in an individual learning about the violent death of a close family member or friend. It can also occur as a result of repeated exposure to horrible details of trauma such as police officers exposed to details of child abuse."[20]

For simplicity, throughout this book we primarily focus on and use the term secondary trauma (rather than vicarious trauma or PTSD) when referring to the potential negative effects of exposure to graphic and emotionally charged content – in other words, the trauma experienced by others that we may witness online. And although some experts believe that primary trauma can also result from viewing traumatic material, we mainly explore the potential for secondary trauma.

So what does secondary trauma *feel* like? The Office for Victims of Crime (OVC) in the U.S. Justice Department explains that over the long term, secondary trauma responses can be positive, negative, or neutral. Those responses can also mimic those of trauma itself: "While individuals respond to vicarious trauma in a number of ways, *a change in their world-view is considered inevitable* – people can either become more cynical or fearful, or they can become more appreciative of what they have, or both."[21] Negative responses may include difficulty managing emotions, emotional numbness, sleep challenges, decreased resistance to illness, and more. Positive responses may include what's called "vicarious resilience," deriving new strength from proximity to the strength of survivors.

Thankfully, as we explore later, exposure to traumatic events – whether online or off, direct or second-hand – does not automatically result in disorder. A number of "protective factors," which range from the biological to the psychological, social and environmental, can strengthen us and prevent ill effects.[22] And if we do acquire trauma-related symptoms, there are ways to mitigate them.

Most often, experts say, our emotional responses to graphic or distressing content do not add up to secondary trauma, even when those responses are visceral. Indeed, graphic content often evokes our most common, natural, and healthy human

[18] "What Is Posttraumatic Stress Disorder?," American Psychiatric Association, at www.psychiatry.org/patients-families/ptsd/what-is-ptsd

[19] M. A. Crocq and L. Crocq, "From Shell Shock and War Neurosis to Posttraumatic Stress Disorder: A History of Psychotraumatology," 2 *Dialogues in Clinical Neuroscience* 47–55 (2000).

[20] "What Is Posttraumatic Stress Disorder?," American Psychiatric Association, at www.psychiatry.org/patients-families/ptsd/what-is-ptsd

[21] "What Is Vicarious Trauma?" Office for Victims of Crime website, at https://ovc.ojp.gov/program/vtt/what-is-vicarious-trauma

[22] Carl C. Bell, "Exposure to a Traumatic Event Does Not Automatically Put a Person on a Path to Develop PTSD: The Importance of Protective Factors to Promote Resiliency," Gift from within Website.

responses, such as sadness, anger, and empathy. Naming and expressing these emotions can be a critical way of managing them.

Certainly, the definitions above don't lend themselves to neat packages, often spill over each other, and require further scientific exploration. The upshot, however, is that we can have a significant and even life-altering response to traumatic events, even if those events are experienced second hand, through a device in our palms, on a computer screen in our offices, or from the retellings of friends, colleagues, and even strangers. Our responses may not signal or be defined as secondary trauma. Yet awareness of our potential responses – including the most extreme possibilities – and how to protect ourselves from the worst of those potential responses, can keep us safer.

Indeed, awareness of what's happening in our bodies and brains goes a long way toward helping us develop "resilience," defined as an ability to respond to trauma exposure in ways that minimize the risk of long-term negative effects. To foster resilience, we can cultivate internal tools that enable us to ride out the emotional toll of an event without becoming overwhelmed or subsumed by it. Resilience can be both an individual trait or a collective, community-wide phenomenon. Resilience practices may include exercises aimed at "self care," like meditation or yoga, but are also inclusive of deeper structural, cultural, and organizational responses. In addition, the lessons of "positive psychology," pioneered by Martin E.P. Seligman and other researchers, can help us identify the most productive ways to engage with atrocities in our newsfeed, including how we can derive meaning and even growth from connecting with the trauma of others.[23]

* * *

Reporter Haley Willis is a harbinger of how modern-day newsrooms are shifting from an old-school, "toughen up-or-get-out" attitude when it comes to reporting on horrific human events and beginning to embrace processes that are more respectful of journalists' humanity. Immediately after her work on the George Floyd story, Willis admitted, "I'm tired. I'm not sleeping well. I'm having a hard time getting myself to stop working. And I recognize that. Sometimes you can't always take a break, but you should check in with yourself, know your physical and emotional state and what may have changed, try to reposition yourself in the work to address those changes. And … tell yourself that it's *okay* to feel affected."[24]

Willis wasn't always this savvy about how she engaged with graphic content – the potential for being adversely affected by the videos, photographs, and social media posts popping up on her phone and laptop – and how to keep from being overwhelmed by the material. She arrived at UC Berkeley in northern California from Dripping Springs, Texas, a rural town of less than 6,000 people outside of Austin,

---

[23] Martin E. P. Seligman, *Flourish* (New York: Simon and Schuster 2013).
[24] "Alumna's Skills Assist New York Times' Alarming George Floyd Video," *Berkeley News*, June 4, 2020.

in fall 2016. Half Asian and half white, she was keenly aware of being different from her peers in the predominantly white and conservative community in which she grew up. This awareness fueled her participation in human rights letter-writing campaigns while in high school, engaging her with conflicts and atrocities across the globe and sparking a desire to study at UC Berkeley, an academic community historically committed to civil rights and social justice.

Willis was a college freshman, thinking of majoring in sociology, when she saw a job ad for a student to work on a book related to the investigations of war crimes written by Eric Stover, Victor Peskin, and Alexa Koenig. Alexa reviewed her application and suspected she'd be a fit for a slightly more tech and advocacy focused effort that she was about to help launch at UC Berkeley's Human Rights Center: a digital investigations lab for online fact-finding through which students would identify and verify social media and other online content for human rights researchers, investigative reporters, and human rights lawyers. When offered a spot, Willis immediately said yes.

"Growing up in the 2000s, I was an Internet kid," said Willis. "And you kind of [inherently] understand the value of [the Internet]." She quickly recognized the potential power that online information could bring to human rights work. In September 2016, she joined an intensive multi-day immersion into this new world of digital open-source investigations – investigations that use information that is publicly accessible on the Internet – hosted at UC Berkeley by the Human Rights Center and Amnesty International. The project, she learned, sought to bring human rights investigations into the twenty-first century by training students how to mine social media for information and potential evidence of war crimes. Almost by definition, that meant exposing participating students – mostly young adults between the ages of 18 and 25 – to disturbingly graphic content.

During her first week of training in a small classroom on the ground floor of Berkeley's law school, Willis and some forty of her peers analyzed multiple videos of potential evidence of human rights violations in Syria: images of cluster munitions fired at Syrian civilians, taken by Syrian civilians and media activists; fathers and mothers crying out as they searched through the rubble of their homes for lost family members; halted breathing and snippets of Arabic as local youth with camera phones watched in fear and shot videos of planes dropping bombs on the horizon.

Amnesty International's Sam Dubberley, Milena Marin, Scott Edwards, and Christoph Koettl (who now works with Willis on the Visual Investigations team at the *New York Times*) showed students how to use satellite imagery to corroborate the location of the videotaped attacks. Given an online information environment that is rife with misinformation and disinformation, videos are only usable for human rights documentation if they can be verified: if someone analyzes the footage and confirms that the footage is likely authentic and that it shows what it purports to show. So that's what the students were trained to do: find and corroborate images of human rights atrocities.

Amnesty's investigators taught the Human Rights Center students how to mine the Internet to find these user-generated videos. As importantly, they taught students how to become more aware of the potential adverse psychological effects that could be derived from viewing these kinds of images, as well as methods for protecting themselves. Dubberley – who had conducted some of the first research into how user-generated content was affecting human rights researchers and journalists – brought this sensibility to the work. Without his insistence on the importance of this focus, this vital aspect of *how* open-source investigations are best conducted may have been overlooked and a push-through-it culture may have persisted.

Willis soaked up the training and within weeks was watching and verifying videos of the Syrian conflict for the team's partners at the non-profit Syrian Archive. But even with training that sensitized her to the emotional toll of viewing documentation of atrocity, Willis felt the effects. She and her fellow students were encouraged to talk about the Syrian videos and other violent imagery, to cultivate an awareness about the potential effects on them, and to take adequate breaks from viewing the content, among other strategies. Talking with peers, however, didn't help at first, she said, because it gave her a "bit of tunnel vision" about "normal" reactions to the content. She had heard that watching the videos of atrocities could disrupt sleep or lead to nightmares. Willis wasn't having that problem. She was sleeping – a lot. "I was sleeping early, napping a lot. I didn't connect my reaction to the work because in some ways I was having the 'wrong' reaction.'" She eventually realized that sleeping so much and at such odd times was not normal for her and may actually have been a reaction to the violent and disturbing videos she was seeing in her work. Human Rights Center staff encouraged her to take a break for a few weeks. She did so and returned with what she described as greater self-awareness.

Several years into her human rights investigations at UC Berkeley, Willis had a reaction of a different kind. She was walking down Oxford Street near the Berkeley campus and its Center for East Asian Studies, when she saw the remains of a razed building. "I immediately thought, it's a building that has been bombed out," she recalls. That experience led her to realize how deeply she could still be affected by the nature of her work. "It seeps into your daily life and your mind." It was a valuable lesson in the importance of caring for herself in the face of analyzing distressing content – a lesson that has persisted into her professional life.[25]

Six years later, when we interviewed her for this book, Willis (see Figure I.3) was living and working in New York City, a journalist on one of the most lauded news teams in the world, covering the most salient global events. Not only was she continuing to think about how to protect herself from the effects of examining such

---

[25] According to Willis, "Resiliency and dealing with vicarious trauma are probably the most valuable experiences I came away with from the [Investigations] lab." Gretchen Kell, "Alumna's Skills Assist New York Times' Alarming George Floyd Video," *Berkeley News*, June 4, 2020.

FIGURE 1.3 Reporter Haley Willis smiles with an event badge referencing her new position at the *New York Times.*
Source: Photo by Alexa Koenig

graphic content, but was also thinking through how this content might affect the public. It's one thing for journalists to watch raw footage in preparation for a story. But it's another thing for journalists, as gatekeepers, to decide what kinds of graphic content should be shared and exactly *how* those images should be shared.

The video of George Floyd's killing is a perfect example – and for Willis and her team was a test – of whether and if so how to publish disturbing content. Although the Floyd video was being widely viewed by people in the immediate hours after the murder, sparking protests nationwide, Willis's team at the *New York Times* still had to determine what to do with the footage. Her senior producers on the story, Whitney Hurst and David Botti, determined that the Visual Investigations team should work on the story, since there was more to tell than what was already circulating online.

"If we're going to be publishing material that is graphic, traumatizing, especially to a particular group of people who have been watching videos of people who look like them being killed for years, it has to be additive," said Willis. "I can't tell you how many times we've passed on a video of a police killing that for lack of better words is very black-and-white. This case felt like the more we realized small details [in what had been previously reported] that were major, major mistakes, it told a massive story about the accountability of [police] officers. People can say a lot of things like, 'The officers didn't know [George Floyd had stopped breathing]' or 'They didn't have the medical training' but when you listen to the police scanners you realize that they upped the code to an emergency call. This is clear evidence that the officers had realized it was a medical emergency, and yet [Officer Derek Chauvin] continued to kneel on [Floyd's] neck."

Hurst, Willis' co-senior producer on the *New York Times*' Visual Investigations team, was pivotal in deciding how to approach the story. As a Black woman, Hurst said, the video had personal resonance. She told us that she was "without the adjectives" to describe what it felt like to watch the video of the murder. Although there have been photographs of lynchings and other violence against Black people through history, this video represented another level of documentation. From the get-go, she wanted to see if her team could bring "a bigger understanding" to the events depicted in the video by looking critically at the official police narrative.

As graphic, raw footage flies around the Internet, journalists, like Willis, Hurst, and their colleagues at *The New York Times*, are needing to ask this very difficult question: When does it advance understanding to spotlight videos like that of George Floyd's murder, and when is it gratuitous? And what adverse psychological effects will amplifying such a video have on viewers in general or particular segments of the community?

"My favorite response [from the public] after we published [our investigation into George Floyd's murder] was, 'I thought I knew what happened and I didn't,'" said Willis. The story in the *New York Times*, published five days after the murder, relied on bystander videos, surveillance videos, and on-the-ground reporting to give a step-by-step account of what happened, including what officers did and did not do. "That for me was proof that we made the right decision in pursuing this story – it revealed something about what the officers did and why it was wrong." Three days after *The New York Times* published its piece on Floyd's killing, three other officers who had been present at the scene faced charges of aiding and abetting second-degree manslaughter and second-degree murder.

While it's not the job of journalists to protect viewers from disturbing material when it reveals what is going on in the world, reporters often factor in the potential effects on viewers. Christoph Koettl, who joined the *Times* newsroom in 2017, told us that he regularly thinks about the impact of his newsroom's reporting on the public. "We really strive to analyze [a] video and provide context and use that footage to provide some added value and insight," said Koettl.

Koettl (see Figure I.4) explained that his newsroom had similarly grappled with what to do with footage from other atrocities given its graphic nature, such as a 2018 chemical weapons attack in Douma, Syria. Taken by an aid worker, footage he viewed showed children foaming at the mouth and struggling to breathe in the wake of the attack. Koettl said several of his team members felt strongly that the *Times* shouldn't run the video, "especially of children," as what's called b-roll – the background footage that plays while reporters speak on camera. In the end, the newspaper decided to black out everything in the visuals except pertinent details, such as the eyes affected by the chemicals, because showing all of the details was simply too disturbing and not additionally informative.

FIGURE 1.4 *New York Times* reporter Christoph Koettl speaks to UC Berkeley students about his team's visual investigation into a US drone strike that killed an innocent man and his family members in Afghanistan.
Source: Photo by Alexa Koenig

Hurst said that the *New York Times* newsroom and her team in particular are always considering how to approach a story and what kinds of footage to use, and she goes into these editorial decisions with a "tremendous amount of humility" and openness to how people may perceive those decisions. Since Floyd's killing, for example, she said, other people of color have been murdered or abused by police with images caught on camera and their reporting team hasn't always used the footage – especially if the footage depicts a horrible event but isn't itself likely to advance the public's understanding of what happened. Of course that doesn't stop motivated viewers from seeking out the raw footage online.

Following the Floyd investigation, Hurst and a colleague came up with guidelines for their department on how to treat this kind of violent footage and then discussed their ideas with fellow journalists. Hurst said the guidance includes asking such questions as: Should we show the footage? How will the victim's family perceive it? What's the news value? What additional context needs to be provided? In deciding whether to pursue a visual investigation or to use a video, Hurst said she asks, "So why do we need to show it? If we don't have to show it, let's not show it," which she acknowledged "sounds weird for a video person to say." She underscored that adding a video of how someone was killed doesn't necessarily honor them or push a story in a new direction.

Koettl's advice for people who may come across graphic images and struggle with their reactions? "Number one: it's okay to be upset if you read or watch the news. But on the other hand, it's important to not let your life be consumed by it."

* * *

As Dr. Rachel Naomi Remen has said: "The expectation that we can be immersed in suffering and loss daily and not be touched by it is as unrealistic as expecting to be able to walk through water without getting wet. This sort of denial [of our experiences] is no small matter. The way we deal with loss shapes our capacity to be present to life more than anything else. The way we protect ourselves from loss may be the way in which we distance ourselves from life and help. We burn out not because we don't care but because we don't grieve. We burn out because we've allowed our hearts to become so filled with loss that we have no room left to care."[26]

The pages that follow are ultimately about navigating this line: avoiding the risks of secondary trauma while meaningfully engaging with the often violent and painful news of our times. As humans who are inextricably connected to each other and our surroundings, we must find effective and sustainable ways of witnessing and grappling with each other's trauma in order to dismantle the systems of violence and oppression of which we are all a part.

[26] Rachel Naomi Remen, *Kitchen Table Wisdom* (New York: Macmillan 1996).

1

A Short Summary of a Long History
of Graphic Witnessing

It was 1963 and Josiah Thompson was perplexed: In one hand, he held a *Life Magazine* article that suggested President Kennedy, who had recently been assassinated, had been shot from behind. In his other hand, he held a *New York Times* article that suggested Kennedy had been shot through his throat. The forensic evidence to back those conclusions – from the medical reporting to the photos and the videos of the infamous event – couldn't be reconciled. As Thompson has written, what he did next made "even less sense" than the apparently contradictory information in the articles. He walked to a nearby FBI office to point out the discrepancy. He said the agent listened politely, took down his name, thanked him for his comments, and then likely "had a good laugh."[1]

The young, self-appointed investigator of the Kennedy assassination was dismissed out of hand – for a time. As Thompson details in his book *Last Second in Dallas*, the perplexing questions he raised of how many shots were fired and the direction from whence they came launched a nearly six-decade-long inquiry into Kennedy's killing (Figure 1.1). The careful work Thompson did for *Life Magazine* in the 1960s – conducting a frame-by-frame analysis of bystander Arthur Zabruder's video, which captured the moment of Kennedy's murder[2] – has been highlighted by *New York Times* journalist Christoph Koettl as one of the most notable visual investigations of the twentieth century. Five decades later, visual investigations of a similar nature, ones that rely heavily on videos and photographs posted to the Internet, are often hailed as "new" by organizations like the *New York Times*, *Washington Post*, *BBC Africa Eye,* and the citizen journalist collective known as Bellingcat[3] – although as

[1] Josiah Thompson, *Last Second in Dallas* (University Press of Kansas 2021): 6–7. This apparent contradiction in the evidence started Thompson's multi-decade inquiry into Kennedy's killing, including an investigation into how many people were likely involved in the assassination and whether there was more than one shooter.

[2] The *Life* article was later expanded into Thompson's first book, *Six Seconds in Dallas: A Micro-Study of the Kennedy Assassination* (Bernard Geis Associates 1967).

[3] Christoph Koettl, Daragh Murray and Sam Dubberley, "Open Source Investigation for Human Rights Reporting: A Brief History," in Sam Dubberley, Alexa Koenig, and Daragh Murray (eds),

FIGURE 1.1 Private investigator Tink Thompson, at his home in northern California, reflects on his visual investigation of the assassination of President John F. Kennedy, while Andrea Lampros listens and looks on.
Source: Photo by Alexa Koenig

Thompson's investigation makes clear, in several ways, they aren't. While the science may have improved and the tools may have changed (shifting from analog to digital), many of the traditional methods of scrutinizing the visual documentation of historic moments remain.

However, it's not just the visual investigation methods that have been inherited by contemporary generations: As Thompson has acknowledged, painstaking examinations of photos and videos like the graphic shots of Kennedy's killing, whether taken by news organizations or members of the public, could be difficult to digest. Ultimately, all of us who are bombarded with images of some of the worst things humans do to each other face the risk *and opportunity* of being forever changed by that exposure – in ways that can be good, as when inspired to band with others to create positive social change, or bad, as when facing down the specter of secondary trauma.

Photographic witnessing can take many forms, ranging from the work of professionals charged with documenting urgent events and sharing that news with the world; to everyday people who become accidental witnesses to atrocities and capture their experiences on smart phones and upload those images to the Internet in

Digital Witness: Using Open Source Information for Human Rights Investigation, Documentation and Accountability (Oxford University Press 2020): 12.

order to inspire awareness; to activists who deliberately capture and curate images to inspire action; and even to videos and photographs shared by perpetrators who may disseminate images to instill fear in others, to brag about their exploits, or to recruit people to their cause.

In the following text, we describe several iconic images that have entered the collective consciousness and serve as cultural milestones. The descriptive summaries may be upsetting given the detail we provide of the graphic violence they depict and the often racialized and gendered nature of the violence. However, we felt they were important to include as illustrations of points woven throughout this book about how graphic images can both harm and heal. While each of these images has played a role in helping to make sense of our world, many of them are also notable for having inspired and ignited social change.

✳ ✳ ✳ ✳ ✳

1863, Louisiana: Peter stumbled into the Union encampment in Baton Rouge, his clothes "ragged and soaked with mud and sweat,"[4] smelling of the onions he had rubbed across his skin to throw off the bloodhounds that had been chasing him.[5] For ten days and nearly eighty miles, he had run barefoot across Louisiana, escaping a slave plantation and carrying with him the scars of a vicious whipping that had confined him to bed for two months and nearly claimed his life.

During his medical examination in the camp, the doctors exposed the scars that crisscrossed his back like tree roots. According to one account, the scars "sent a thrill of horror to every white person present, but the few Blacks who were waiting … paid but little attention … such terrible scenes being painfully familiar to them all."[6]

A photograph of the moment, commonly ascribed to William D. McPherson and J. Oliver, became possibly the most famous photo of the Civil War. Later labeled "The Scourged Back," McPherson and Oliver's photo was converted into a *carte de visite*,[7] something like a thick postcard, and widely disseminated, spreading across the country and eventually landing in the pages of the nation's most popular magazine *Harper's Weekly* (where Peter was, instead, called Gordon). The photograph was used to counter Southern slaveholders' insistence that slavery is humane. At the same time, there were cries of "fake news" issued by a group known as the

---

[4] Erin Blakemore, "The Shocking Photo of 'Whipped Peter' That Made Slavery's Brutality Impossible to Deny," *History*, May 11, 2021.

[5] Frank H. Goodyear, III, "The Scouraged Back: How Runaway Slave and Soldier Private Gordon Changed History," America's Black Holocaust Museum, available at: www.abhmuseum.org/the-scourged-back-how-runaway-slave-and-soldier-private-gordon-changed-history/ (last visited June 16, 2022).

[6] *New York Tribune*, December 3, 1863, available at: www.newspapers.com/image/78661360/ (last visited June 16, 2022).

[7] David Silkenat, "'A Typical Negro': Gordon, Peter, Vincent Colyer, and the Story Behind Slavery's Most Famous Photograph," 15 *American Nineteenth Century History* 169–186 (2014).

"Copperheads," an organized political movement comprised of Northerners who were sympathetic to the South and supportive of slavery.

The photo would go down in history as one that "excited both the sympathy and indignation of every humanitarian that has seen it," becoming a cornerstone of the abolition movement, and praised as greater than words in its power to motivate action. The photo allegedly inspired several Black people to join the Union Army and prompted previously neutral whites to support the abolitionist cause.

1943, Warsaw: A little boy of elementary school age is dressed in a newsboy cap, overcoat, knee socks and laced up boots, hands raised in surrender, a cluster of children and women behind him, hands also up. The little boy's face is a mask of fear. Men in rounded helmets and uniforms stand to the side of the group, one looking toward the women and children while his machine gun is directed toward the boy, a slight smile on his lips.

Although this photo would become one of the most infamous of the Holocaust, it remains of indeterminate origin. The person who captured the picture may have been a bystander, a perpetrator, or a professional but was most probably a member of Propaganda Company 689, a unit of the German army then stationed in Warsaw. The boy has never been identified, but the man possessing the machine gun and the smile is Josef Blosche, the Schutzstaffel's (SS) Rottenfuhrer or "section leader." Blosche and his unit had just discovered some of the last hideouts in the Warsaw Ghetto while attempting to squelch the "largest act of Jewish resistance against the Holocaust." The woman and child, along with the other women and children in the photo, would soon be sent to the Treblinka and Majdanek extermination camps.

The image would make its way into a photo album prepared by SS General Jurgen Stroop, who oversaw the operation, as a souvenir gift for Nazi party leader and Holocaust architect Heinrich Himmler. Three leather-bound copies were ultimately made: one for Himmler, one for Stroop, and one for Friedrich-Wilhelm Kruger, chief of the SS and the police in Krakow, Poland, along with an unbound "file" copy that remained in Warsaw. Images from the photo album, later referred to as the "Stroop Report," would eventually serve as evidence of SS crimes in the Nuremberg trials. In 1945, the *New York Times* published the image alongside others from the report, but the photo didn't become widely known until the 1970s, with several manuscripts later written about the haunting image.

According to Richard Raskin, who wrote a key book about that moment, the photo was interpreted quite differently by SS troops than by those who suffered during the Holocaust or by the general public who later viewed it: "One set of men saw in that photograph heroic soldiers combating humanity's dregs while the vast majority of mankind sees here the gross inhumanity of man."[8] Ultimately, as we discuss later in this book, the photo is a searing illustration of how personal and context-bound our interpretations of photographs can be.

[8] Dan Porat, *The Boy: A Holocaust Story* (Hill and Wang 2011).

FIGURE 1.2 Mamie Till, held by her future husband Gene Mobley, looks at her son, Emmett Till, lying in a morgue. Mamie Till insisted her son's funeral be open casket so the world would have to confront how brutally he'd been killed. Her actions are credited with helping to strengthen the US Civil Rights Movement.
Source: Photo by David Jackson, published in *Jet* Magazine. (Courtesy of the National Museum of African American History and Culture, Smithsonian.)

1955, Chicago: As explained in the Introduction, Mamie Till Bradley refused to heed admonitions to close the casket of her fourteen-year-old son, Emmett Till, who lay before her, his face swollen and disfigured, just as it had been in the morgue. (see Figure 1.2). Emmett had been visiting relatives in Mississippi when he allegedly flirted with the white married proprietor of a grocery store. While the woman had reportedly refrained from telling her husband, news in the small town traveled fast. Her outraged husband and half-brother hunted the boy down, pulling him from his bed in the small hours of the night – kidnapping, beating, and mutilating him before shooting him in the head, tying a cotton-gin fan around his neck with barbed wire, and tossing his body in the Tallahatchie River.

Three days later, two boys were fishing when they discovered Emmett's body. The beating and the water's wear had left the boy unrecognizable; an engraved ring on his finger, though, helped with identification. When the child's body was sent home to his family in Chicago, his mother insisted on a public funeral, daring the thousands of people who attended to confront how the country had failed her son. *Jet* Magazine first printed the photo of Mamie viewing Emmet's body; other publications quickly spread the images of Emmett's swollen face, drawing critical attention to the extraordinary cruelties of American racists and the culture and systems that had bred them.

FIGURE 1.3 Three fraternity brothers from the University of Mississippi Kappa Alpha chapter pose with guns next to a bullet hole–ridden memorial sign for Emmett Till. Source: Courtesy of the Mississippi Center for Investigative Reporting

The acquittal of the murderers in 1955 by an all-white Mississippi jury was met with understandable outrage, if not surprise. As originally reported in the *New York Times* and as recounted by Allissa Richardson in her book *Bearing Witness While Black*, jurors rendered their verdict in just an hour and five minutes, with one telling reporters, "If we hadn't stopped to drink pop it wouldn't have took [sic] that long."[9] The defendants would later confess to the brutal murder in a magazine interview, but they never faced legal justice, protected initially by their white privilege and later by the US legal principle of double jeopardy, which prevents second prosecutions for a crime. Despite the lack of legal reckoning, the photos of Emmett in his casket did motivate a form of *social* justice: Widespread outrage, ignited by obvious injustice and fanned across Black media, many believe, was a critical catalyst that helped launch the modern Civil Rights Movement.

While Emmett's story – and the visual representation of his murder – is now more than sixty years old, the underlying narrative is far from over. In July 2019, on what would have been Emmett's seventy-eighth birthday, a second photo went viral. Three young white men stood with guns in front of the historical marker that commemorates the spot where Emmett's body was found along the Tallahatchie River, the sign pockmarked by bullet holes[10] – a visceral reminder of cruelty and racism and how, if not addressed, such behavior can surge across generations (Figure 1.3).

9 Allissa Richardson, *Bearing Witness While Black: African Americans, Smartphones, and the New Protest #Journalism* (Oxford University Press 2020): 10.
10 Michael Quander, "This Picture of Students with Guns at Emmett Till Memorial Went Viral. Now People Are Having Conversations about Racism," *Kare* 11, August 1, 2019.

FIGURE 1.4 Nine-year-old Kim Phuc, center, otherwise known as "Napalm Girl," running down Route 1 near Trang Bang, Vietnam, after the United States–ordered aerial napalm attack on June 8, 1972.
Source: Photo by Nick Ut, Associated Press

1972, Vietnam: A young girl, arms spread wide like wings, runs toward the camera, her eyes squeezed closed, mouth open, and howling (Figure 1.4). Slate-colored smoke obscures the road behind her, an ominous backdrop to the girl as well as to the four other children and five soldiers captured in the black-and-white photo. Some have twisted their heads around as they run, looking over their shoulders at whatever horror they're fleeing.

The girl depicted in the foreground was Kim Phuc, nine years old that day in 1972 when her village was napalmed by the South Vietnamese under orders from a US commander. The napalm, in the words of a National Public Radio (NPR) account, "incinerated her village, her clothes, and then, her skin,"[11] which began peeling off her body. Nick Ut, a photographer for the Associated Press, snapped the photo and then scooped up Kim (who passed out from her burns), taking her and a number of other children to a hospital.[12] When medical workers initially declared her beyond help, he demanded they treat her. She survived.

The Associated Press published the photo despite their initial hesitation. Technically, the picture violated their editorial prohibition against nudity, but the importance of documenting the true horrors of the conflict – and the very human costs of that conflict – ultimately trumped any concern they had with showing a young girl naked. The image quickly became a national focal point that according to NPR "transcended the divisive debate about the rights and wrongs of the Vietnam War and crystallized the barbarity of war."[13] It has been credited with raising widespread support for bringing that conflict to an end.

[11] "'Napalm Girl': An Iconic Image of War Turns 40," *NPR*, June 3, 2012.
[12] "Story Behind the Terror of War: Nick Ut's 'Napalm Girl' (1972)," About Photography Blog, October 26, 2019.
[13] "'Napalm Girl': An Iconic Image of War Turns 40," NPR, June 3, 2012, available at: https://wamu.org/story/12/06/03/napalm_girl_an_iconic_image_of_war_turns_40/ (last visited June 16, 2022).

FIGURE 1.5 Screenshot from a video captured by George Holliday on March 3, 1991, which shows Rodney King being beaten by police.
Source: Photo is in the public domain

More than forty years later, the image would once again become news. In 2016, a Norwegian author named Tom Egeland posted the Pulitzer Prize–winning photo to his Facebook page, only to have Facebook's content moderators suspend his account and remove the post for violating its policy on nudity. The censoring triggered widespread outrage across Norway, reaching everyone from staff at Norway's largest newspaper to the prime minister,[14] eventually sweeping much of the globe.

After initially defending its actions, Facebook backed down. Critics pointed out that Facebook and other social media platforms had by that time become a prominent source of news for much of the world; not allowing socially important graphic content meant limiting the world's access to the kinds of information needed to inform debates and inspire change. Facebook cited a "balancing test" to explain its policy reversal, determining that because the photo was "an iconic image of historical importance, the value of permitting sharing outweighs the value of protecting the community by removal." Facebook promised to update their policies to better "promote free expression" while keeping the public "safe."[15] However, as discussed in Chapter 7, the challenges of appropriate content moderation are ongoing.

1991, Los Angeles: A Black man is curled in a fetal position outside a light-colored car, the driver's door ajar. Four white men in uniforms encircle him. They crouch like athletes prepared for action, somehow leaning both toward him and away as their blows hover, then fall fast (Figure 1.5). As their target struggles to rise, one of the officers begins to swing his baton like a baseball bat, repeatedly hitting the man's shoulders crosswise as if at a low-lying piñata that he's determined to burst. The kicking and beating continue on and off for approximately fifteen minutes.

[14] Abby Ohlheiser, "Facebook Backs Down, Will No Longer Censor the Iconic 'Napalm Girl' War Photo," *Washington Post*, September 9, 2016.
[15] Ibid.

Across the street, George Holliday, awakened by the thump, thump, thump of helicopters and the wail of sirens, ran to his balcony to look down at the commotion below. He grabbed his recently purchased video camera and "instinctively" started filming. "You know how it is when you have a new piece of technology," he later recounted to the *New York Times*. "You film anything and everything."[16]

At first, he didn't know what to do with the footage. Mostly he wanted to know what had happened on his street. Acquaintances seemed disinterested and police wouldn't give him information, so a few days later, he called a local television station to see if they had information. They didn't but were interested in seeing what he'd recorded. That night, KTLA played the footage on the 10:00 pm news, triggering a firestorm of media interest. The police quickly came to the station and confiscated the footage, but the television station had made and kept a copy.[17]

Holliday's footage of Rodney King's beating has been called "the world's first viral video."[18] While King survived, he'd suffered close to a dozen skull fractures, a broken eye socket, and nerve damage across his face.[19] Former California Congresswoman Karen Bass, who represented a large swath of Los Angeles and now serves as its mayor, has said of the footage's release, "Many of us who had been trying to convince the public that these kinds of incidents were happening were almost relieved. It was like finally, finally it was on camera. And the world was going to be able to see and we would finally be able to hold police officers accountable."[20]

Despite the video evidence of what had occurred, a year later – after the trial was moved to a predominately white suburban neighborhood thirty miles outside of Los Angeles that was home to a large number of police officers[21] – one of the four white officers was released due to a hung jury, while the other three officers were acquitted, just as Emmett Till's murderers had been. That night, Los Angeles erupted in anger and frustration. The video had seemed incontrovertible proof of inexcusable violence by police against Black people.

Ilyce Meckler, an investigative producer who worked for Los Angeles PBS Station KCET told us over email, "I first saw the video of LAPD officers beating Rodney King in 1991 on local TV when I was with a colleague working late one night. The low resolution video, shot with consumer equipment, immediately prompted many questions and long discussions within our newsroom. It ultimately led us to embark on a series of related investigations: of the videotape itself, the officers on tape involved in the beating, and how the LAPD handles allegations of excessive

---

[16] Azi Paybarah, "He Videotaped the Rodney King Beating. Now, He Is Auctioning the Camera," *New York Times*, July 29, 2020.

[17] Pablo Ximénez de Sandoval, "Meet the Man Who Recorded the World's First Viral Video," *El Pais*, May 25, 2017.

[18] Ibid.

[19] "30 Years after Rodney King LAPD Beating Video, What Has Changed?," KTLA5, March 30, 2021.

[20] Ibid.

[21] "Timeline: Rodney King and the LA Riots," Southern California Public Radio, available at: https://projects.scpr.org/timelines/la-riots-25-years-later/ (last visited June 18, 2022).

force, misconduct and racism. We also examined how the judicial system handles cases involving law enforcement officers.[22] The camcorder itself, which captured the graphic images, became a unique eyewitness to the events that unfolded."

As she explains, "Obtaining a copy of the beating videotape shot by concerned citizen George Holliday was only the beginning of our long reporting process. The original images, audio and videotape had to be verified and then examined. The audio was enhanced by an acoustic phonetics expert using the latest technology available at the time. For example, racial epithets that some heard on the tape became more audible after helicopter noise was reduced. We also examined more than one hundred pages of public records including criminal and civil court records, police investigative documents and electronic messages sent by the LAPD officers to each other. Our investigative team gathered information that pointed to a history of systemic problems policing the police. We interviewed more than 30 law enforcement officers, officials and dozens of individuals throughout Los Angeles and its many diverse neighborhoods. We covered both the state and federal criminal trials as well as the riots that followed the announcement of acquittals on almost all of the charges in the state case. Timelines and outlines were created to help organize the multimedia material coming from video, audio, court records and our interviews."

The violence that followed the acquittals lasted nearly a week, leaving more than 50 people dead and more than 2,000 hurt. In an attempt to quell the outbreak, Rodney King went on camera, heeding a request to calm the country. Once on camera, however, he set aside the speech that had been written for him and spoke the famous words for which he's since been immortalized: "Can we all get along?"

2001, New York: At 8:46 am on September 11, 2001, a plane flew into the World Trade Center's north tower. Initially believed to be a horrible fluke, the significance of what had just happened would only become clear when a second plane flew into the south tower nineteen minutes later. The second attack was echoed by two more elsewhere: less than an hour later a plane crashed into the Pentagon. Minutes later, another plummeted from the Pennsylvania sky, all four planes having been converted into the simplest of makeshift missiles.[23]

Moments after the second plane hit the World Trade Center, a man inside peeled himself from the carpet where he'd been thrown and stumbled toward his office door, only to slip on broken glass. "That's when I turned and realized that [the office] window had blown in. The columns in the wall had stayed, but nothing else. I was open to the sky, 89 stories in the air. I was stunned at how blue the sky was."[24]

For the people below, that blue sky was now pockmarked by a terrifying rain of concrete, airplane parts, and human bodies. And nearly 3,000 people from 62 countries lay dead or dying.

[22] Email from Ilyce Meckler to Alexa Koenig on May 11, 2022 (on file with the authors).
[23] See, for example, Damon DiMarco, "Timeline of Events," *Tower Stories: An Oral History of 9/11* (Santa Monica Press LLC 2009).
[24] Ibid.

FIGURE 1.6 A hooded man standing on a box, arms spread, wires protruding from his fingers, and disappearing beneath his cloak. One of many photographs taken in 2004 documenting torture perpetrated by US personnel at Abu Ghraib Prison.
Source: Photo is in the public domain

One photo from that day is particularly infamous: a man in a business suit falling from the Towers head first as if diving, one leg gracefully tucked, his body perfectly aligned with the tower's vertical columns (see Figure 3.1).

With AP photographer Richard Drew's "falling man" picture on September 11, suddenly "a single frame out of hundreds shot in haste"[25] became one of the most controversial in American history. Some lauded it as "one of the most perfect pictures ever taken."[26] However, many major media outlets refused to print it, labeling it too disturbing. Regardless of the reaction, it is now considered one of the most haunting images of the twenty-first century.

2004, Abu Ghraib, Iraq: Just three years later, the world watched in increasing horror as photo after photo of torture at an American military base in Iraq began to flood the media, the United States' promotion of itself as a paragon of human rights and the rule of law chipped away with each image: A photo of naked, hooded men piled on top of each other as a male and female soldier grin behind them; a man leashed and forced to crawl on the floor like a dog; another recoiling against a steel

[25] Richard Drew, "20 Years On, the 'Falling Man' Is Still You and Me," *Associated Press*, September 9, 2021.
[26] Ibid.

door, his hands bound, as a dog lunges toward him, teeth bared; a line of men forced to masturbate as a female sergeant points and laughs; a body sandwiched between two stretchers on which a male sergeant sits casually cross legged as if at kindergarten circle time; a man hooded and cloaked, standing on a small box, arms spread as if in crucifixion, wires protruding from his fingers and disappearing beneath his cloak (Figure 1.6). First released by *Sixty Minutes II*, and later in pivotal pieces by journalist Seymour Hersh in the *New Yorker* and in 2006 in *Salon*, more than one thousand photos and hundreds of videos would collectively paint a horrifying picture of abuse, including clear violations of international and domestic law.

Army Reservist Joe Darby was just twenty-four years old and a few months into his post as a military policeman at Abu Ghraib when a buddy of his, Corporal Charles Graner, slipped him a CD containing hundreds of photos and videos that Graner and colleagues had taken. Initially, Darby laughed when he saw the photos of detainees piled into a human tower, but his smile quickly faded as he scrolled through hundreds of images of torture, including "a video of a uniformed American soldier sodomizing a female detainee, [and] an image of a corpse, its face battered and bruised, bundled in a cocoon of ice."[27]

After weeks grappling with whether to report what he'd seen, Darby slipped an anonymous note and a copy of the CD under the door of the US Army's Criminal Investigations Division, the unit tasked with investigating allegations of military wrongdoing.[28] While the division had promised confidentiality, someone leaked the photos and videos to the press. Shortly after, U.S. Secretary of Defense Donald Rumsfeld went on television, reporting Darby (who was supposed to have remained anonymous) as the source of the images. Rumsfeld's outing of Darby led to death threats against Darby and his wife, who were forced to go into hiding – shifting blame and vitriol from those who had committed the abuses to the whistleblower.

The most widely seen and best known of those photos were taken by Staff Sergeant Ivan Frederick, the man who sat cross-legged on the sandwiched detainee, described above. He, Private Charles Graner, and Private Lynndie England would all serve several years for their crimes, even as those at the highest levels of command who implicitly condoned the abuse avoided accountability. While the legal response was nominal given the severity of the crimes, the images from Abu Ghraib created widespread awareness of the United States' deviation from the rule of law and its illegal embrace of torture as a tactic of war.

2014, Tahrir Square, Egypt: A young woman – naked and bloodied – stumbles as the men surrounding her shove and tug at her, the lone police officer and handful of women trying to protect her no match for the mob. Earlier that day, crowds had gathered in Tahrir Square in Cairo, Egypt, to celebrate the inauguration of

---

[27] Eric Stover, Victor Peskin and Alexa Koenig, *Hiding in Plain Sight: The Pursuit of War Criminals from Nuremberg to the War on Terror* (University of California Press 2017): 349.
[28] Ibid. at 352.

President Al-Sisi. But the event turned violent, erupting in what are known as "circles of hell":[29] packs of men, sometimes numbering in the hundreds, who surround a woman and perpetrate mass rape, including the gang rape of this woman.[30]

Normally, an event like this would receive little international attention, given the relative ubiquity of such circles and the lack of documentation. At least eighteen other women were similarly raped that day.[31] But on June 8, 2014, a video of this particular rape surfaced on YouTube. The event as captured by the amateur video triggered global outrage. Twelve men would ultimately face trial for the assault, something that likely wouldn't have happened without the viral video and the attention it attracted.[32] As discussed in Chapter 7, the video also set off heated debates within YouTube about whether such videos should be kept online given their potential newsworthiness and social value, or removed in light of the woman's privacy interests, the graphic nature of the content, and the potential psychological harm to the public from witnessing such violence. It would also spur important conversations among the growing but nascent community of human rights activists who document atrocities with online content, triggering questions of consent over using such sensitive video and the imperative to bring light to horrific events, while minimizing the potential trauma for the victim at the center of the crime.

2020, Minneapolis: George Floyd's head and shoulders are all that can be seen as he lies prostrate behind a police car, eyes closed. A white man in a blue shirt kneels on his neck, the black of the man's pants bleeding into the dark brown of Floyd's bare skin. The cop stares straight into the camera recording him, his hands stuffed into his pockets as if this is a casual encounter. But his defiant glare and parted lips betray emotion that simmers just below the surface, and he keeps his knee pinned to Floyd's neck even after Floyd stops breathing.

This time, the viral video of police brutality wasn't shot by a forty-something-year-old man as in the case of Rodney King, but by a seventeen-year-old girl, Darnella Frazier. Parallels between her video of George Floyd's killing and Holliday's video of King's beating are obvious, with both documenters serving as unintended witnesses to acts of outrageous cruelty. But this time, the video that enters the legal record as evidence will result in a conviction, the officer guilty of murder.

Today, Frazier grapples with the effects of the role she played in alerting the world to a shocking crime – the crime of police abuse that plays out across the United States, often without documentation, multiple times a week. Forced to leave her

---

[29] Amnesty International, *Egypt: Token Reforms Fail to End Scourge of Pervasive Violence against Women* (January 21, 2015).

[30] Malsin 2014.

[31] "#TimeToAct: Hania Moheeb Was Sexually Assaulted In Tahrir Square," SkyNews, June 10, 2014.

[32] Madeleine Bair, "Consent, Privacy, and Video of Sexual Assault," Witness Blog, available at: https://blog.witness.org/2014/06/consent-privacy-video-sexual-assault/; Madeleine Bair, "Navigating the Ethics of Citizen Video: The Case of a Sexual Assault in Egypt," *Arab Media & Society* (Issue 19, Fall 2014).

FIGURE 1.7 A strike on a bridge in Irpin in March 2022 killed a woman, her two children, and a volunteer.
Source: Photo by Lynsey Addario for *The New York Times*

home because it was no longer safe due to the extensive publicity of her role in spot-lighting the role of the police in the crime, she has suffered from panic and anxiety attacks, as well as sleeplessness. And the trauma has extended beyond her, to her nine-year-old cousin who was with her, to her family who has helped her grapple with the aftermath, to the many who remotely viewed her video, and with it, Floyd's death. Speaking out on Instagram on the one year anniversary of Floyd's murder, she explained: "Even though this was a traumatic life-changing experience for me, I'm proud of myself. If it weren't for my video, the world wouldn't have known the truth. I own that. My video didn't save George Floyd, but it put his murderer away and off the streets. … These officers shouldn't get to decide if someone gets to live or not."[33]

2022, Irpin, Ukraine: Two soldiers crouch over the body of a young man, check-ing for signs of life (Figure 1.7). Their focus on this man – blood splattered across his face and hand – is an indicator that the people curled next to him on the asphalt are already gone. Just behind his shoulder is a little girl in a puffy blue jacket and red pants; behind her a woman in a pink coat lies on her side encircling her purse as if protecting it in sleep, her head resting against the sidewalk. At the rear, a young man in a navy jacket lies behind a navy suitcase – both fallen on their side as though ready to continue their journey, if just made vertical.

A soldier with a Ukrainian patch on his arm watches the huddle of soldiers and the dead in dismay. Behind them, an older man with a backpack takes a long stride off the sidewalk, his eyes avoiding the bodies, as if intent on pressing forward. Framed against the pale gray sky, a bronze statue of a soldier in a World War II uniform backdrops the bodies, a chilling reminder that Europe has witnessed scenes like this before.

---

[33] Joe Hernandez, "Read This Powerful Statement from Darnella Frazier, Who Filmed George Floyd's Murder," *NPR*, May 26, 2021.

Earlier that morning, Tetiana Perebyinis had loaded her parents and her two children – Mykyta, 18, and Alisa, 9 – into the family minivan and set out for Kyiv.[34] After two days hiding from artillery fire in the basement of their apartment in the suburb of Irpin, she had decided it was time to evacuate.

That same morning, *New York Times* photojournalist Lynsey Addario, Ukrainian journalist Andriy Dubchak, and their security advisor, Steve Bungay, had set out for Irpin.[35] Addario had seen photos of civilians fleeing across a collapsed bridge to escape the Russian advance and set out to see what was going on. The suburb had become a site of heavy fighting as Russian forces advanced from Hostomel and Bucha just to the north.[36] Airstrikes, indiscriminate artillery fire, and targeted executions had forced civilians into hiding and then compelled many to take their chances by crossing the destroyed bridge and flooding out of the city for safety.

When Addario and her team arrived, they hid behind a cement wall, watching as civilians, assisted by Ukrainian soldiers, streamed across the bridge. Artillery and small arms fire peppered in the distance. Addario described the scene to *The Daily* host, Michael Barbaro:

> There was a Ukrainian mortar position off in the distance. So I assumed, OK, the [Russians are] targeting the Ukrainian mortar position. And so I said to myself, in my head, everyone knows this is a civilian evacuation route. There's no way they're going to target civilians. … And it was well-known, very visible from the other side, from Irpin, that there's civilians coming.

Soon after Addario and her team took their position, Tetiana and her family made a break for it. After driving their minivan as far as it could go, they needed to clear the final stretch of exposed street on foot. Led by twenty-six-year-old church volunteer Anatoly Berezhnyi, the family dashed out. But just as they did, a Russian mortar struck, in full view of the team from the *Times*.

The photo Addario shot of Tetiana, Anatoly, Mykyta, and Alisa lying dead in the street – then unidentified – was printed the next day on the front page of the *New York Times*. The *Times* does not normally publish images that feature the faces of the dead, but this photograph illustrated a potential war crime, frozen in time, as few could. It was through this photo that Tetiana's husband, Serhiy Perbyinis, learned of his family's death. And in its relatability to families across the world, it became emblematic of the horrific suffering of Ukrainian civilians under attack from Russia and further hardened much of the world's determination to support Ukraine.

---

[34] Andrew E. Kramer, "They Died by a Bridge in Ukraine. This Is Their Story," *New York Times*, March 9, 2022.

[35] The Daily, "The Story Behind a Defining War Photo," March 15, 2022; "Civilians Hit by Russian Shelling While Fleeing Irpin," available at: www.gettyimages.com/detail/news-photo/new-york-times-security-advisor-steve-bungay-drags-a-man-to-news-photo/1384235234.

[36] Siobhán O'Grady and Max Bearak, "After Weeks of Street Battles, Kyiv Suburb is Scene of Ruin," *Washington Post*, April 3, 2022.

IMAGES AND ACTIVISM: WHAT'S DIFFERENT TODAY?

The videos and photographs now circulating in our media share a legacy with these iconic images in contributing to an awareness of what is happening in the world, and in some cases, prompting action. From the viral photo of Peter and his scars, which helped rally new supporters to the abolition movement of the 1860s, to the video of the assault on George Floyd, which helped fuel the Black Lives Matter movement of the early 2020s, to the killing of Ukrainian civilians, which has helped rally near-global support for Russia's target, images shared across contemporary media – whether captured by professionals or amateurs – have the potential to inspire communities, catalyze action, and motivate change.

Thousands of refugees fleeing the war in Syria and conflict or economic violence in Africa had already died in transit in the Mediterranean region in 2015 when professional photographer Nilüfer Demir took a photograph that would stop the world: A two-year-old Syrian boy, in a short-sleeved red top and blue shorts, his tummy peeking through, shoes still on his baby feet, lying face down in shallow water on the shores of Turkey. We learned that the boy's name was Alan Kurdi, and that he and his mother and five-year-old brother had died when an inflatable plastic boat bound for the Greek Island of Kos capsized.

Suddenly the war in Syria and its resulting refugee crisis was collectively felt, as witnesses imagined or recalled the visceral ache of losing a child. It was rare for a photo of a dead child to be published in mainstream media. The photo went viral, inspiring record donations to refugee organizations, and leading several countries, such as the UK, to accept more Syrian refugees. The phenomenon prompted researchers and news organizations to wonder aloud why some photographs have the power to humanize and activate a response while startling statistics – millions of displaced, hundreds of thousands of deaths – and other types of photos do not.

In an interview, the photographer Demir spoke of his heavy, mixed emotions about the photo:

> On the one hand, I wish I hadn't had to take that picture. I would have much preferred to have taken one of him playing on the beach than photographing his corpse. What I saw has left a terrible impression that keeps me awake at night. Then again, I am happy that the word finally cares and is mourning the dead children. I hope that my picture can contribute to changing the way we look at immigration in Europe, and that no more people have to die on their way out of a war.[37]

While graphic videos and photographs have repeatedly proven their power to trigger organizing and other types of response, user-generated content brings with it a rawness that can hit people differently than professional media. Seldom trained in journalistic ethics and techniques designed to protect the psychological well-being

---

[37] Ismail Küpeli, "We Spoke to the Photographer Behind the Picture of the Drowned Syrian Boy," *Vice News*, September 4, 2015.

of the viewer and the dignity of the person depicted, smartphone users pass around images they've generated whose content is often selected *for* its graphic and even shocking quality – a quality harnessed to motivate a reaction. Often, it's the most salacious, the most damning visual images that are shared across social media and "go viral."

It's this rawness, this sense of authenticity, that gives open-source content tremendous power. As Susan Sontag has noted in the context of the public's reaction to photos from World War II, "the photographs of Bergen-Belsen, Buchenwald, and Dachau taken in April and May 1945 by anonymous witnesses and military photographers seem more valid than the "'better' professional images"[38] because of where they fall across the spectrum that spans from "life" to "art." As she has explained, "Beautifying is one classic operation of the camera, and it tends to bleach out a moral response to what is shown. Uglifying, showing something at its worst, is a more modern function: didactic, it invites an active response. For photographs to accuse, and possibly to alter conduct, they must shock."[39]

Few if any better understand the power of shocking images to support social justice than Eileen Clancy, a New York video archivist and co-founder of I-Witness Video, an organization she established in 2000 to try to bring relevant videos taken by everyday people to the attention of lawyers working to protect peaceful protestors from prosecution and hold police to account for their misconduct.[40] From New York to Belfast, Clancy has been on the cutting-edge of thinking through how to harness modern technology in the hands of citizens who are on the frontlines of social change – such as video cameras and smartphones – and how to get these user-generated images into courtrooms to strengthen civil litigation, and especially, criminal defense.

Clancy started her career in activism in the 1980s, joining the growing solidarity movement with Central Americans struggling for basic human rights in the midst of Cold War politics. In the 1990s, she expanded her work to document police violence in New York and in her mother's homeland of Ireland, sharing videos with lawyers in an effort to exonerate those wrongfully detained and charged.

At a protest outside of an IMF World Bank meeting in Seattle in 1999, organized to bring attention to human rights abuses spurred by globalization, police systematically attacked protesters with tear gas and arrested nearly 500 people. Clancy witnessed this afar via the Internet, noting the massive scale of police abuse and the police's growing militarization, including their donning of elaborate armor that up until then had rarely been seen in the United States. Given her experiences in Northern Ireland, she recognized this type of gear and military-grade weapons as an inflection point in the policing of nonviolent protests.

---

[38] Susan Sontag, *Regarding the Pain of Others* (Picador 2003): 77.

[39] Ibid. at 81.

[40] Mark Andrejevic, "Watching Back: Surveillance as Activism," in Sue Curry Jansen, Jefferson Pooley and Lora Taub-Pervispour, *Media and Social Justice* (Springer Link 2011): 180–181.

A year later, at IMF-World Bank demonstrations in Washington, DC, Clancy similarly noticed that many demonstrators and independent filmmakers were using hand-held video cameras to document what was happening. This gave her immense – but temporary – relief because she figured there would be ample footage of the police overreach. She assumed that this documentation would help ensure that justice prevailed, until she realized that those cameras were largely held by people who would simply walk away with the footage.

That's when Clancy and her co-founder decided to merge forces to establish the non-profit collective I-Witness Video. "All these people are [wrongfully] coming up on police charges, but there's no counter to what the police are saying," Clancy said. She and her colleagues organized themselves to either generate or acquire video evidence, process the evidence archivally, and then analyze it, ultimately supplying the most helpful footage to lawyers. "We had to think about 'Well, what do you need to capture, what needs to be in the scene?' We had to be able to predict what the police would do and what the activists would do because the goal was to get to the place where you could film what actually occurred."

Decades before Darnella Frazier would spontaneously capture George Floyd's death, Clancy and her team began deliberately documenting police misconduct around the Republican National Convention held in Philadelphia in 2000 and New York in 2004. Clancy said that in 2000, police used raids to harass potential documenters. In 2004, Clancy and others from I-Witness Video documented protests during which more than 1,800 people were arrested. Over the following year, approximately 400 cases would be resolved or thrown out solely because of video evidence. According to Clancy, this is because the sworn police statements that accompanied the cases included statements so far removed from the facts evidenced in the video, prosecutors had to toss the cases out.

In 2008 in St. Paul, Minnesota, just before the Republican National Convention began, police raided the rented homes of Clancy and her team, presumably in an effort to intimidate them, kicking in the doors and holding those present at gunpoint. When the team released footage of the raids, even greater attention was attached to Clancy's work.[41]

Eventually Clancy and I-Witness Video's efforts to train activists to videotape violence began to pay off. Although the video footage from handheld cameras was often "crummy," Clancy said, her team determined that entire tapes should be turned over to lawyers, keeping working copies for themselves. The footage would not be edited by the activists or anyone first, in order to preserve the videos' forensic value. Clancy's first major win came in the context of the 2000 Republican National Convention in Philadelphia when her team turned over video footage of an activist who was across town from where police alleged he had committed a crime.

---

[41] Democracy Now! "I-Witness Video Collective Forced Out of Living Space after Second Raid by St. Paul Police in Five Days," September 4, 2008.

According to Clancy, "The whole allegation was a farce." Thanks to the footage, the case against the activist was thrown out. The activist later brought a civil suit against the police and won. "This was a person who was heavily targeted," Clancy said. "And we kicked ass."

Clancy is one of many who have noticed the qualitative differences between citizen imagery and professional reporting. "There was this fantasy that you can just give people camcorders and you'll get the same thing [as professional capture]; you just can't." They are, in the end, two different phenomena. Until, that is, professional journalists started integrating user-generated content into their own reporting, selecting and embedding the raw material in a more analytical context, the analysis helping viewers to process the visuals emotionally by helping make sense of what they were shown.

Today, we are seeing vast differences in how open-source content is used (or not used) by the media. Ashley Bradford is a former-archivist-turned-investigative technologist who worked with a team of UC Berkeley students to create a digital tool to help minimize the risks of exposure to traumatic video content. Bradford explained how traditional newspapers and television news programs starkly differ from social media platforms in choosing what content to feature: "Anything potent is dangerous. ... It's important to keep in mind that [online] content is built for eyeballs: things that are abnormally scandalous, or violent or far fetched are meant for clicks; [social media sites] are not objective news sources. They are ad-selling machines, and they are selling eyeballs."

Of course, the differences between citizen imagery and professional imagery aren't only qualitative, they're also quantitative. The volume of lay imagery compared to professional imagery can be huge, as can the volume of digital imagery compared with earlier, analog eras. Whereas war reporters once generated a few hundred shots from which only a handful might be selected for publication, today's online spaces can bend under the weight of thousands of videos and photographs of a single incident or event – easily developed and distributed at a volume and pace that would have been previously unimaginable. While newspapers and television stations had a relatively constrained number of pieces they could produce each day given page and time limitations, by 2020, more than 500 hours of videos were being uploaded to YouTube each minute, alongside 350,000 posts created on Twitter, and 243,000 photos uploaded onto Facebook. This means that the general public can now be exposed to graphic imagery at a scale never previously experienced.

And then there's a third difference between citizenry imagery and professional reporting, beyond the qualitative and quantitative differences: differential access to events. When it comes to some situations, professionals may capture much of what we see, for example, when they're given exclusive access to the scene of a crime or embedded with a military unit. But when it comes to random events that occur in public, whether in times of war or peace, that's where everyday people are more likely to capture an atrocity simply because they may happen by some spontaneous event and be equipped with a camera on their smartphone or otherwise. In this, it is neither the quantity of images any person takes nor the quality of the images that captures the difference, but simply the likelihood of being at the wrong place at the right time. Of course, there are also hybrid circumstances, where a professional happens to be present at an historic event, for example, Richard Drew photographing the man falling from the World Trade Center.

Clancy's career as an activist and archivist has ultimately served as a bridge from the analog world to the digital, which has made many of these differences (quantitative, qualitative, and access based) possible. Clancy still remembers a breakthrough moment in the early 1990s that allowed user-generated video to be shared and played on computers: "We got QuickTime, a Mac IIci, and we put the CD-ROM [of a video] in there, we were very excited. And this little thing opens up and it's like an inch square and robotic. I was like "this?!?! This postage stamp?!?" It was important, it was symbolic, but it was thirty years from what we can do now. We knew where it was going to go (in a sense), we could see it, but we could not get there."

For good and bad, though, here we are. Today, we not only have video that we can capture on devices that we can carry in our pockets, but (as we discuss in Chapter 7) virtual reality that can immerse the viewer in a 3D replica of world events, placing them at the algorithm-induced yet highly realistic center of a fire, a war zone, or other crisis. Ultimately, Clancy's early steps paved the way for the work being done on award-winning visual investigations teams at the *New York Times*, *Washington Post*, *Associated Press*, and elsewhere. These teams analyze raw footage often shot by ordinary members of the public, and based on that analysis, piece together videos and photos to tell a story that illuminates what transpired – stories that simply can't be told with words alone. Stories like George Floyd's killing.

2

Images and Our Bodies

It's not the bloody, graphic imagery that gets to Sam Dubberley, a veteran human rights investigator and former journalist. Over ten years working in broadcast news, including three years as the head of Eurovision News Exchange, he was consistently on the front lines of graphic content, reviewing footage from conflict zones and human rights crises during the tumultuous Arab Spring and the onset of the Syrian conflict, digitally witnessing some of the most heinous things human beings can do to each other. He was pretty stoic about it – for a time.

Dubberley told the journalists on his team at Eurovision, some older and some younger, that they didn't have to watch the videos of beheadings in Iraq by insurgents. *He* would watch the videos in order to report on, analyze, and verify what had happened. He could handle it. "Handling it" meant repeatedly watching a video that showed the beheading of twelve men lined up in a row, with the last man able to hear and see the murders of the eleven before him. Nobody wiser or more experienced stepped in or even cautioned Dubberley about the potential effects of watching these violent crimes on his computer screen. Fifteen years later, the images are still seared in his brain.

But even those worst-of-humanity images weren't the worst for him. Dubberley remembers covering a massacre at the Beslan school in Russia's North Caucasus region in 2004. Over three days, Chechan terrorists occupied the school, taking hundreds of children, teachers, and parents hostage. A Russian siege of the school resulted in the deaths of 360 people, including 186 children. In his mind's eye, Dubberley can still see the children running out of the school, terrified and nearly trampling each other. "It has not been the gore that's affected me," said Dubberley. "It's the inhumanity – or the missing links of humanity – of it. It's not the airstrike that kills the kid. It's the parents crying in the hospital afterwards."

Through 2010 and 2011, the height of the Arab Spring, the twenty-five journalists on Dubberley's team covered news around the clock. For the first time in history, people in the middle of a conflict had smart phones and could upload images nearly instantaneously to the Internet for the world to see. The work of combing through and analyzing videos, photos, and social media posts from that period was especially hard on the few Arabic speakers who were expected to watch and translate the material for Western media.

Not knowing much about the effects of this exposure to violent footage and without a vocabulary to discuss secondary trauma, but recognizing that he and his teammates were feeling acute distress from the work that included shifts in world outlook and an increase in concerning behaviors, such as excessive drinking, Dubberley reached out for expert support. He contacted a psychologist who had counseled members of the Irish police after their investigation-related exposure to child pornography – images that are known to be especially distressing – and asked the psychologist to talk with his team to provide expert mental health support. The young journalist made the psychologist's sessions compulsory for his newsroom. Although some of the most hardened reporters, especially those who had covered conflict in the Balkans, would claim "I'm fine, I'm fine," Dubberley later heard that the stories about disturbing or graphic news events flowed freely at the pub alongside the beer – and sometimes even tears – at the end of the day.

Were the emotional responses that Sam Dubberley and his newsroom colleagues experienced indicative of direct trauma, secondary or vicarious trauma, or simply sadness, hopelessness, or anger?

As the scientist Robert Sapolsky explores in his book *Behave: The Biology of Humans at Our Best and Worst*,[1] this question should be viewed through a multidisciplinary lens involving biology, neurology, psychology, and more, to comprehend what happens in our brains and bodies when we witness something distressing. What's happening neurologically shouldn't be boiled down to static definitions from any particular discipline, he says. And yet, knowledge of the biological and psychological gears that may be turning in our bodies and brains when we view graphic or other upsetting online content may help us work with, interrupt, or at least better understand our reactions.

Unlike Dubberley and other journalists on the digital front lines, most of us aren't spending the bulk of our workday watching beheadings, scrutinizing bomb attacks, or unraveling strings of hate-filled misinformation. And yet, a "breaking news" message may pop up on our cell phone while we are serving breakfast to our kids to alert us of a mass shooting. If we click on a link, we could be taken to a scene of sirens, of people fleeing a crisis, of blood, and of anguish. As we pour syrup on our waffles or usher our kids to school, we might be caught off guard as the normal events of our lives juxtapose with the horrific events occurring in someone else's life. Images may catapult us to the massacre at Sandy Hook Elementary School in Newtown, Connecticut, or to an attack on a crowded outdoor café in Paris, or to a murderous event even closer to wherever we call home. Understanding what's happening in our brains may inform how we take in and process this content – not to turn away from it, but to be aware of how it is affecting us. Even with the numerous differences

---

[1] Robert Sapolsky, *Behave: The Biology of Humans at Our Best and Worst* (Penguin Press 2017).

that lead us to be more or less triggered by other peoples' pain, some basics of brain processing unite us.

At least three parts of our brain, the amygdala, hippocampus, and cortex, are affected in overlapping ways when we witness traumatic events, whether experiencing that event first or second hand, via a person's verbal account, video footage, audio recordings, or written materials. These parts of our brain are components of our limbic system, which controls our emotions and behavior and which comes into play when we have an emotional response to an event and form a memory of that experience. Sapolsky explains that the limbic system regulates our autonomic nervous system (also called our involuntary nervous system),[2] which has two parts: the sympathetic nervous system that tells us when to fight or flee, and the parasympathetic nervous system that helps us calm down.[3]

When we're exposed to something "sufficiently terrifying," Sapolsky says, our limbic structures impact our brain and our bodily functions.[4]

Veronica O'Keane, author of *A Sense of Self: Memory, the Brain, and Who We Are,* calls the amygdala the "emotional sparkplug" of the brain; while it does not *create* emotions, it kickstarts our emotional response.[5] The amygdala fields feelings like sadness, fear, joy, and anger through our neural pathways, calibrates a response, and issues the orders for flight, fight, or freeze.[6] The amygdala releases hormones when stimulated: Adrenaline fuels a response and cortisol helps channel that response. In the right amounts, these hormones produce clarity of thought; in excess, they overwhelm.

The cortex, by comparison, heads up our executive functioning and manages emotional reactions from a more measured place. Each of our senses has its own real estate on the cortex – sight, sound, smell, taste, and touch pathways deliver sensations via neurons.[7] While not an emotional center like the amygdala, the cortex is still a repository of senses and ultimately plays a huge role in helping us make sense of and make meaning from experiences.

The hippocampus, situated in the temporal lobe on both sides of our brain, connects the amygdala and the cortex and, researchers say, provides the link between memory and learning. Can't remember what you had for lunch yesterday, but can remember what summer smells like in your hometown? That's your hippocampus. Even before neuroscience explained the connection between smell and memory,

---

[2] Ibid. at 27.
[3] Ibid. at 26.
[4] Ibid.
[5] Veronica O'Keane, *A Sense of Self: Memory, the Brain, and Who We Are* (WW Norton 2021): 69.
[6] Some researchers have identified a fourth response, "fawning," which includes becoming helpful and compliant to the person posing a perceived threat. See, for example, Sherry Gaba, "Understanding Fight, Flight, Freeze and the Fawn Response: Another Possible Response to Trauma," *Psychology Today,* August 22, 2020, available at: www.psychologytoday.com/us/blog/addiction-and-recovery/202008/understanding-fight-flight-freeze-and-the-fawn-response.
[7] O'Keane, *A Sense of Self,* 34.

the writer Marcel Proust captured this phenomenon in his famous description of a madeleine (a little French cookie) soaked in tea, with a scent that somersaults the protagonist to his childhood. This "Proust Effect"[8] is a much over-cited and yet useful example of how our olfactory system (which hits our amygdala first) connects with our memories (situated in our cortex) to make meaning (a mash-up, courtesy of the hippocampus).

The hippocampus, Veronica O'Keane says, is a key player in the process of recovery from trauma and in minimizing these effects because it combines information from past experiences to assemble our response to a later event. We need the hippocampus to help us imagine and anticipate, to fret, and to foresee.[9] The hippocampus sends the amygdala a signal to indicate when a traumatic event is over. If it is not doing its job of containing a traumatic experience to a specific time and place, we may never get the memo that the trauma is over. Flight and fight remain in play. Hormones continue to be released. And the effects of trauma (directly or indirectly) continue unabated.

Now to the point of how these parts of the brain function together in response to provocative videos, photos, and other content.

Frank Ochberg is a psychiatrist and catalytic force behind the Dart Center for Journalism and Trauma, an organization that addresses the potential mental health toll of reporting and offers strategies for developing resiliency. Ochberg underscores that exposure to trauma and the process of recovering from traumatic experiences is in part biological: Trauma has been shown to alter the relationships among the frontal cortex, the amygdala, and the hippocampus.[10] This is a key component of post-traumatic stress disorder (PTSD) – or what Ochberg prefers to call post-traumatic stress injury (PTSI). He uses the term PTSI to emphasize that what people experience in the aftermath of exposure to trauma isn't a disorder so much as the effects of an understandable, ongoing injury to the brain – and thus is a term that is more "accurate, hopeful and honorable."[11] "What I keep pointing out is that PTSI is real," said Ochberg. "This is not just in somebody's head. It's as real as having diabetes or having atrial fibrillation. There is an organic change. We're learning more and more about it. It helps to have medical doctors appreciate the condition and treat it."[12] Ochberg and others describe how the brains of those with PTSI or some other residual trauma experience look different than the brains of people

---

[8] Cretien van Campen, "The Proust Effect: The Senses as Doorways to Lost Memories," Oxford Scholarship Online (2014).

[9] David Eagleman, *The Brain* (Pantheon 2015).

[10] Larry Abbot, "Art, Trauma, and PTSI: An Interview with Dr. Frank Ochberg," 28 *Journal of Military and Veterans' Health*, October 2020, available at: https://jmvh.org/article/art-trauma-and-ptsi-an-interview-with-dr-frank-ochberg/ (last visited January 12, 2022).

[11] Matthew Friedman, Elana Newman, and Frank Ochberg, "PTSD v. PTSI: More than a Name," *Dart Center for Journalism and Trauma*, October 1, 2012.

[12] Abbott, "Art, Trauma, and PTSI."

without such experiences on imaging tests, especially in the gray matter, almost like they have a scar.[13]

Our reaction to trauma dwells in this limbic system or what some psychologists describe as our "reptilian brain," which controls our most primal responses and desires. As the limbic system developed in humans, the cortex got more involved in compartmentalizing and stemming reactions and our more primal brain was tamed. Even though we have this "new brain" that helps manage our behavior, however, our reptile brains are still lurking and firing off alarm signals.[14] Sapolsky says the cortex communicates with the limbic system but doesn't necessarily reign in emotions.[15]

It is the relationship between trauma and memory that is key to how we're affected long term. *New York Times* reporter Ezra Klein interviewed Bessel van der Kolk, author of the bestselling book *The Body Keeps the Score*, about the connection between trauma and memory and how the effects of trauma can persist:

> [T]rauma is really a wound that happens to your psyche, to your mind, to your brain. Suddenly you're confronted with something that you … faced with horror and helplessness. That nothing prepares you for … and you go like, 'Oh my god.' And so something switches off at that point in your mind and your brain. And the nature of trauma is that you get stuck there. So instead of *remembering* something unpleasant, you keep *reliving* something very unpleasant. … So the job of over-coming trauma is to make it into a memory where your whole being knows this happened a long time ago, it's not happening right now. But the nature of trau-matic stress is that you keep reacting emotionally and physiologically as if these events are happening right now.[16]

Let's step back to how we might take in a traumatic video – say of a police shoot-ing. Some information just flows through our brains, never to be seen or heard or remembered again. For some of us, that's the content of our eighth-grade chemistry class or the name of the novel on our bedside table. However, some information – traveling through the brain as neurons – finds kindred neurons and locks arms, increasing the odds that we'll remember the moment and respond to future trig-gers. O'Keane says that short-term memories form when cells "fire together for long enough to become wired together" – and once they are wired together through a process called "consolidation," the memories stick with us. So if we associate a video with a previous experience of police violence or even with a previously viewed graphic video that affected us, the experience could be more profound and likely more disturbing.

---

[13] "How Does PTSD Affect Brain Function?," available at: www.giftfromwithin.org/html/brain-function-webcast.html.
[14] Interview by the authors with Dr. Wendy Kirk on January 15, 2022.
[15] Sapolsky, *Behave*, 28.
[16] Ezra Klein and Bessel van der Kolk, "This Conversation Will Change How You Think about Trauma, The Ezra Klein Show," August, 24, 2021, podcast audio, available at: https://podcasts.apple.com/us/podcast/the-ezra-klein-show/id1548604447.

UC Berkeley professor Ronald Dahl, director of the Institute of Human Development, founding editor of the journal *Developmental Cognitive Neuroscience*, and a developmental neuroscientist and pediatrician, talks about that loop of worry and rumination that causes people to get stuck replaying an image, trying to work through it. "Like sticking your tongue in a toothache, it hurts but you can't stop doing it," explains Dahl.

When it comes to replaying traumatic videos in one's head – such as the video of George Floyd's killing – that replay becomes part of what Dahl calls the "dysfunction trajectory," or a cycle of negative thoughts. Dahl says young kids are often relatively immune to the dysfunction trajectory but become more susceptible after puberty thanks to hormonal and neurological shifts. The replay is the signature of rumination; it traps you in a never-ending cycle, often occurring as you're trying to fall asleep or when you wake in the middle of the night.

Unfortunately, conscious efforts to *not* think about upsetting material often back-fire. As reflected in the title of the book by the linguist George Lakoff, once you hear the phrase "don't think of an elephant" an elephant is all you can think of: Once you tell someone not to think about something, that something becomes almost impossible to set aside.[17]

Researchers say anyone – from the general news-reading public to journalists to human rights investigators – can suffer from secondary trauma due to their exposure to the trauma of others and that there can be neurological and physiological similarities between experiencing trauma first hand and second hand. *The Atlantic's* Aaron Reuben reported on this relationship between trauma and trauma exposure in "When PTSD Is Contagious," a discussion of the experience of secondary trauma in the wake of 9/11. He reported that "second-line responders to tragedy – humanitarian workers, therapists, social workers, lawyers, and journalists – can develop traumatic stress disorders that mimic the PTSD of their clients, patients, and sources, down to the images of violence that can haunt a traumatized mind."[18] Reuben recounts the story of a psychiatrist who asks his medical students and doctors to imagine a lemon:

> 'Hold it in your mind,' he says, 'See how yellow it is. Smell the citrus aroma. Now cut a slice off with a knife and take a bite. Taste the strong sour flavor.' When he asks people to raise their hand if they are salivating, nearly all do so. The point of the experiment is simple: What you think and imagine can result in a demonstrable, physical reaction. When a therapist for a patient with PTSD hears a story of violence, empathetic imagining can inadvertently trigger a physiological reaction similar to what the victim may have experienced: a racing heart, shaking hands, nausea, and other elements of the fight-or-flight response.[19]

[17] George Lakoff, *Don't Think of an Elephant: Know Your Values and Frame the Debate – The Essential Guide for Progressives* (Chelsea Green Publishing 2004).

[18] Aaron Reuben, "When PTSD Is Contagious," *The Atlantic*, December 14, 2015.

[19] Ibid.

UK researcher Pam Ramsden, in 2017, presented "Vicarious Trauma, PTSD and Social Media: Does Watching Graphic Videos Cause Trauma?,"[20] at the 3rd International Conference on Depression, Anxiety and Stress Management, discussing the potential for social media users to acquire vicarious trauma from viewing social media posts depicting "devastation and destruction." Defining vicarious trauma as "the transfer of violent, traumatic experiences from client/patients to a person of a helping profession," she concluded that general populations are being indirectly affected by viewing such content. She evaluated four clinical studies of people who were "significantly affected by … events" that they had only witnessed via social media and found that of the study participants approximately 20 percent scored high on clinical measures of PTSD, even though they had no previous trauma experience and had only experienced the events online.[21] One of Ramsden's studies, which included 189 men and women with an average age of 37, found that 22 percent of participants "scored highly on clinical assessments of PTSD, despite only being exposed to videos and images of the traumatic events, not the events themselves." The researchers also found that the more times the participants viewed particular content related to traumatic events, the more affected they appeared to be.[22]

These findings parallel the results of a 2015 survey, among the first of its kind to focus on the effects of working with digital content related to human rights violations. The research, conducted by Sam Dubberley, Elizabeth Griffin, and Haluk Mert Bar, consisted of an online survey of 209 journalists and human rights researchers who were exposed in the course of their work to digital content, such as graphic videos or photographs of war or conflict, often uploaded onto smartphones and posted on the Internet.[23] Forty percent of participants reported that this exposure had resulted in high or very high "personal adverse effects," such as changes in sleep patterns, outlook on the world, and effects on relationships. Twenty percent said their exposure had resulted in high or very high "professional adverse effects," including having to take long-term sick leave or quitting their jobs.[24]

New York University researcher Meg Satterthwaite and colleagues uncovered similar findings in their 2018 study of human rights advocates, "Trauma, Depression,

---

[20] Pam Ramsden, "Vicarious Trauma, PTSD and Social Media: Does Watching Graphic Videos Cause Trauma?," 3rd International Conference on Depression, Anxiety and Stress Management, *Journal of Depression and Anxiety* (2017).

[21] Ibid.

[22] "'Trigger Warning': Violence on Social Media Can Cause PTSD-Like Symptoms," Medaxs, May 26, 2015.

[23] Sam Dubberley, Elizabeth Griffin, and Haluk Mert Bal, "Making Secondary Trauma a Primary Issue," Eyewitness Media Hub (2015), available at: http://eyewitnessmediahub.com/uploads/browser/files/Trauma%20Report.pdf (last visited July 17, 2022).

[24] In this study, "professional adverse effects" means that the exposure affected the respondent's work performance.

and Burnout in the Human Rights Field."[25] One of the first international surveys of its kind, the study looked at all types of exposure to trauma (online and offline) and found that 19.4 percent of those working with traumatic content were experiencing things like intrusive memories, sleep changes, weight gain or loss, or increased irritability consistent with PTSD and depression. Nearly 19 percent experienced "subthreshold" PTSD, indicating that they displayed some PTSD symptoms. Just as concerning, the researchers found that 83 percent of participants had little to no access to counseling about how to minimize the negative impact of their human rights work on their psychological well-being.

In the fifth edition of the *Diagnostic and Statistical Manual of Mental Disorders (DSM)*, published in 2013, the American Psychiatric Association affirmed that viewing traumatic imagery can result in negative psychiatric effects, including secondary trauma. However, the *DSM* limits its findings to workplace exposure, refusing to consider whether ordinary people can suffer similarly in the course of scrolling through news feeds.

While the potential for developing negative physiological responses from viewing extremely distressing content has been repeatedly acknowledged by researchers, the question of whether we can *unsee* something disturbing remains. Back to Sam Dubberley: Can he erase the memory of watching a series of beheadings in a video twenty years ago? Neuroscientists say that by and large we cannot erase our memories, but we can interrupt how the amygdala, cortex, and hippocampus triage a traumatic event to ensure that memories don't stick around quite so easily.

In the journal *Molecular Psychiatry*, researchers highlighted a way to interrupt unwanted images that persist following a traumatic event, such as a car accident.[26] Researchers studied whether "cognitive tasks with high visuospatial demands will selectively disrupt sensory (predominantly visual) aspects of memory" in the window of time before memories are "consolidated."[27] In this case, study participants were car crash survivors in a hospital emergency room who were asked to play the video game Tetris, which involves racing a timer while trying to move shapes around quickly to fit into a pattern, to see if the activity would disrupt intrusive memories in the week following the accident. Researchers found that playing the game within six hours of the trauma did result in fewer upsetting memories.[28] Researchers studying Tetris have found that the visuospatial game can increase the volume of the hippocampus to both improve memory and disrupt or weaken the memory of a

---

[25] Sarah Knuckey, Margaret Satterthwaite, and Adam Brown, "Trauma, Depression, and Burnout in the Human Rights Field: Identifying Barriers to Resilient Advocacy," 49 *Columbia Human Rights Law Review* 267 (2018).

[26] L. Iyadurai, S. E. Blackwell, R. Meiser-Stedman, et al., "Preventing Intrusive Memories after Trauma via a Brief Intervention Involving Tetris Computer Game Play in the Emergency Department: A Proof-of-concept Randomized Controlled Trial," 23 *Molecular Psychiatry* 674 (March 28, 2017).

[27] Ibid. at 674.

[28] Ibid. at 678.

traumatic event.[29] But is this disruption only effective immediately after a traumatic experience? Other researchers showed an aversive film to 54 study participants, used the Tetris task four days later, and found that the activity similarly resulted in fewer intrusive memories.[30]

In Chapters 3–6, we explore how research on memory, on the relationship between primary and secondary trauma, and on the positive and negative effects of witnessing graphic material in our newsfeeds plays out. We'll see that although we share biological functions, our socio-emotional lives differ, making us more or less vulnerable to adverse effects from viewing violent images. We'll look at the "protective factors" that, Frank Ochberg says, promote resilience. And we'll make some recommendations for how we can take action – like turning on something called a "savoring channel" – to take in traumatic content in safer and potentially more meaningful ways.

---

[29] Osin Butler, Kerstin Herr, Gerd Willmund, et al., "Treatment and Tetris: Video Gaming Increases Hippocampal Volume in Male Patients with Combat-Related Posttraumatic Stress Disorder," 45 *Journal of Psychiatry Neuroscience* 279 (July 1, 2020).

[30] Muriel A. Hagenaars, Emily A. Holmes, Fayette Klaassen, and Bernet Elzinga, "Tetris and Word Games Lead to Fewer Intrusive Memories When Applied Several Days after Analogue Trauma," 9 *European Journal of Psychotraumatology* (October 31, 2017).

3

Images and Identity

While our brains go through similar processes when confronting distressing social media content, what we find distressing varies. How and when those processes are triggered and how we respond can differ significantly depending on context: the nature of what we encounter, what our past experiences have been, what coping mechanisms we use, our political persuasions, and even the reasons why we are looking at a particular video or photograph in the first place. Reactions to distressing imagery are almost never a one-size-fits-all. When we talk about what is distressing, we need to talk about distressing *to whom*.

For Eileen Clancy, the video archivist and activist introduced in Chapter 1, "Who you are equals how you respond." To illustrate her point using an offline example, Clancy told us the story of a white woman who was arrested and jailed in New York City after a protest. The conditions in the jail, a converted bus terminal, were notoriously bad. Clancy explained that the woman shared a racial identity with the predominantly white police force and therefore didn't think they would mistreat her. She was sorely mistaken. "[The woman] has her period, she needs to use the restroom, needs tampons, needs whatever she needs, she goes to the cops and they don't care. They say no. She tells them, 'This is abuse, you can't do this to me,'" recounted Clancy, who had interviewed the woman for a legal case. "She tells them her brother is in the FBI, that he's in the Joint Terrorism Task Force ... she mentions headquarters down in Queens, etc." to try to get them to identify with her. But the officers continued to ignore her requests. The woman finally became so enraged at her treatment, Clancy said, that she took out her used tampon and threw it at the police officers.

Ultimately, according to Clancy, the woman's distress was less about the officers' refusal to let her use the bathroom than it was about the ways in which this incident damaged her sense of who she was and her identity in relation to others. "I told her there's a spectrum of life-changing stories, [including] a bunch of monographs of women's time in prisons in Northern Ireland. I told her, "Now you're part of that tradition, that history." She was very distraught by that, her changing view of the world."

Susan Sontag, in her seminal book *Regarding the Pain of Others*, has pointed out that while photographs have power in their universality, not being bound to a specific language and thus being accessible to all people,[1] we all derive different meanings from those photographs. As she's warned, "no 'we' should be taken for granted when the subject is looking at other people's pain. ... Normally, if there is any distance from the subject, what a photograph 'says' can be read in several ways."[2] While war photography is often created and published in condemnation of war, Sontag explains that in addition to motivating peace, depending on the identity of the viewer, "surely [the same photograph] could also foster greater militancy."[3] To assume one response, she explains, "is to dismiss politics."[4]

Sometimes, it's less about the graphic nature of imagery than the history a moment carries with it that gets to us – and peoples' relationship to that history, and thus their identities, that determines their differing reactions. The overturn in 2022 of the Supreme Court case *Roe v. Wade*, which for fifty years had protected a woman's constitutional right to an abortion in the United States, is one of these floor-shifting moments where no graphic content is required to stir a deep and unsettling traumatic response. Indeed, sometimes it's not the graphic nature of an image but the monumental nature of the news itself that affects us; that news can feel for some like a boa constrictor wrapped around their chests, squeezing out their ability to take a deep breath. But of course for others, including those who had long labored to eliminate a women's right to choose, that same decision may feel freeing.

University of Southern California Professor Allissa Richardson has described the role she believes identity plays in how we create, how we consume, and the meanings we derive from visual imagery. In her book *Bearing Witness While Black*, Richardson explores visual reporting of the deaths of Black men at the hands of police and how the response to such reporting varies with a viewer's identity:

> As a former full time journalist I sighed every time I saw cable television news loop images of fire and brimstone in Ferguson in 2014, after police killed Michael Brown, or in Baltimore in 2015, after Freddie Gray's death. I wanted someone on air to describe instead how black people experience police brutality, and video proof of it, differently from non-black people. How African Americans, like my father [watching Rodney King's beating] in 1991, see themselves in the bodies of the battered. I wanted the news pundits to say bearing witness while black is a specific kind of media witnessing. It is as networked, collective, and communal as the South African philosophy of Ubuntu, which states, 'I am because WE are.' Black witnessing carries moral, legal and even spiritual weight.[5]

[1] "In contrast to a written account ... a photograph has only one language and is destined potentially for all." Susan Sontag, *Regarding the Pain of Others* (Picador 2003): 20.

[2] Ibid. at 7, 29.

[3] Ibid. at 8.

[4] Ibid. at 9.

[5] Allissa Richardson, *Bearing Witness While Black: African Americans, Smartphones, and the New Protest #Journalism* (Oxford University Press 2020).

"Black witnessing," she has said, ".... involves more than simply observing tragic images on TV or online. It is more complicated than picking up a smartphone and pressing 'record' at the right time. When most African Americans view fatal police shooting videos, something stirs at a cellular level. They want to *do* something with what they just saw. And they want to link it to similar narratives they may have seen before. In this manner, black witnessing is reflexive, yet reflective. It despairs, but it is enraged too."[6]

As she powerfully illustrates, there's a difference in how white and Black populations typically perceive and metabolize images of the killings of Black men, women, and children: "When whites see the videos of [Black men] being brutalized ... they may be able to maintain a safe amount of narrative space."[7]

Of course, such differences in perception aren't just limited to race or ethnicity. Religion, class, and gender are also salient – as are other aspects of our identity. When we asked Liz Scott, who worked as a full-time employee at YouTube in content moderation, whether there was ever a video that she saw that was especially difficult for her personally, Scott answered without hesitation, citing the infamous video of the woman raped in Egypt's Tahrir Square, mentioned in Chapter 1:

> I saw the video before it became news. And I was like 'There's no way [the survivor] wants this public.' But our policy [at YouTube] was not to take this kind of content down. Our policy was this person needs to file a first party privacy complaint [for us to do anything]. So three days later [in response to growing public outrage that the video was still on YouTube] there was a conference for YouTube employees. ... And so sure enough, I get called down to the conference room to go hang out with people more senior than me. They were getting tons of pressure about the video and to take it down. And I was like, *yeah, we should take it down.* It was all men in the conversation except for me. I was arguing we should take this down and the counter was 'but this could spark a social movement in Egypt.' I remember driving to work. I cried every day that week, I was very upset and really felt for this woman. I think for anyone who has had personal experience with sexual assault, you could just so relate to how vulnerable she was in that moment. And I had lived in Egypt, I had been in Tahrir Square. ... My thing was 'no woman should have to be the face of a social movement without her consent.'

All of the videos were eventually removed except for those where the woman's naked body was blurred. Nevertheless, Scott received performance feedback to "not take things so personally" in the future. "I just thought, wow, I'm going to disregard that because this *is* so personal to me."

The link between identity and reactions to what is perceived as challenging has been striking to observe in our work with a very diverse, very international cohort of

[6] Ibid. at 4–5 (italics added).
[7] Ibid.

digital investigators on the Berkeley campus. It was important but perhaps unsurprising that sexual violence survivors would struggle with depictions of rape and harassment; that immigrants and children of immigrants would struggle with slurs leveled against those newly in the country; and that parents would have an especially hard time processing cruelties against children. In such situations, there's an additional, visceral layer of identification with the material beyond that of general human empathy and concern about human rights violations that may be difficult, if not impossible, for others to perceive.

Mallika Kaur, a lecturer who teaches a class on trauma and law at UC Berkeley, underscored that peoples' thresholds of extreme distress can also shift over time. Immediately after she had a baby, for example, she said she was no longer able to watch anything with violence against children, whereas before she could bear it. "I do domestic violence work. I've always worked with trauma, including traumatized children. … But [after having my baby] I couldn't watch any of it." She explained to us how her sensitivity to violence against children became so acute that she got to the point where she would have her husband watch part of a movie for her if it involved children and describe it to her so that she could decide whether she could watch it. She recalled having him watch the first four minutes of one movie in particular, a Punjabi movie that featured the experiences of a parentless child. "I asked, 'Did you cry?' And he was like, 'No, that child [in the movie] doesn't have parents and that's the context for the film but there's no violence.'" Kaur told us she *still* cried when she watched the film, moved by the idea of the child not having parents. "It wasn't graphic, but it was something that resonated so deeply with the enormous responsibility I felt having just brought a child into the world."

Richard Drew, the AP photographer mentioned in Chapter 1 who snapped the iconic 9/11 photo of "The Falling Man," (Figure 3.1) also believes that how we respond to graphic imagery has a lot to do with who we are and what we identify with. He has repeatedly grappled with why media outlets so often refused to print the image of the man in the suit jumping from the World Trade Center, unlike the pictures he took of Robert Kennedy's assassination (which were far bloodier) or Nick Ut's famous photo of the child in Vietnam who had been napalmed and was on fire (an image that was also more graphic). He believes it's because so many Americans can identify with a suited falling man in ways they can't with a famous politician or a foreign child. As he's written:

> In the World Trade Center photo, it's about personal identification. We felt we knew Bobby Kennedy, but we didn't identify with him. We weren't wealthy scions of a political dynasty or presidential candidates. We were just ordinary people who had to show up for work, day after day, more often than not in tall office buildings. Just like the guy at the World Trade Center. … That's what unsettles people about the picture. We look at it and we put ourselves in the jumper's place.

FIGURE 3.1 A person falls from the north tower of New York's World Trade Center on Tuesday, September 11, 2001, after terrorists crashed two hijacked airliners into the World Trade Center.
Source: AP Photo/Richard Drew

While the other photos depict far more visceral pain and suffering, "[t]he man in my picture is uninjured. He does not look like he's in pain. But you know he is moments from death. And you can't help but think, 'That could have been me.'"[8]

Consistently, students in UC Berkeley's Investigations Lab have said that hate speech and violence leveled against people like themselves – in terms of race, gender, sexuality, national origin, ethnicity, etc. – have been especially difficult to process emotionally, even if far less graphic than other posts they may have come across.

For students finding and analyzing social media posts of human and civil rights abuses in countries with which they have family ties, the responses have been mixed, often difficult to anticipate before exposure. For example, one student with family in Syria asked to be moved to a different investigation after several weeks researching Syrian-based war crimes, saying the politics within his family, who supported the Assad regime and whose alleged crimes he was investigating, made the work he was doing psychologically difficult. Conversely, another student, this one with family in Iran, said her inquiry into atrocities in that country was one of the most fulfilling projects she'd ever worked on. For years, she'd heard of her family's suffering but felt helpless to do anything about it; now she had an outlet, the power and agency

---

[8] Richard Drew, "Excerpt: 20 Years on, 'The Falling Man' Is Still You and Me," *Associated Press*, September 9, 2021.

to identify, analyze, and communicate the stories of those victimized to the world which, she hoped, would motivate a response that would protect other potential victims. The meaning she derived from the work was not only protective, but healing.

Another student investigator, this one from Turkey, spent years analyzing images of atrocities from Egypt, Syria, Sudan, and the United States, leading teams to find and verify that information to expose those abuses. Throughout, she experienced little more than expected human reactions to the horrors she witnessed. But when Turkey launched strikes on border towns in northeastern Syria in October 2019, she broke down in front of her team in the middle of a work session. Suddenly, the work she was doing had become too close to home and her distress was spilling over.

What feels "close to home" can be triggered by a variety of identity factors, including gender, race, birthplace, class or geography. "We need "transparency that there *are* people of color doing this work, and what it means to be from the place you're investigating," said another student investigator, whose family comes from Central America. When asked whether there was ever an incident that was especially hard for her to deal with, she explained that "one moment that stood out to me is when I started investigating where I have family, which is Guatemala, and then seeing what people in the U.S. say about people crossing the border from Guatemala. Because of the [Human Rights Center Investigations] Lab, I was able to go to others for support." Having such support from colleagues who are sensitive to the effects of exposure to negative social media about the places and people with whom you identify is critical, she believes, as is providing people with resources like access to therapy or meditation for handling the reactions that come with that exposure.

Michael Shaw is a clinical psychologist, publisher of the website ReadingThePictures.org, and a frequent commentator and writer on visual politics, especially the history and context of images used by the media. As a psychologist, his clientele has included photojournalists and other members of the media. He believes war photographers are more equipped to cope with the violence they witness on assignment because the terror is expectable, and the exposure is for a set length of time. By contrast, "Many conflict photographers living in New York during 9/11 were a lot more unnerved because it happened at home. The same could be seen at the height of COVID as these professionals never expected to see refrigerated trucks filled with bodies in their own backyards."

Ashley Bradford, the technologist working with a team of UC Berkeley students to build a digital tool to minimize exposure to graphic social media content, has also reflected on how who you are affects what content you find triggering online. He's building a digital product that will aid journalists and investigators who have to look at large quantities of graphic content, enabling them to blur disturbing images, mute sound, and tone down other imagery to mitigate the potential of secondary trauma.

"The idea of what can be triggering ... the breadth of that is always surprising to me, even in working with students," he says. "I'm a white guy and haven't had racial slurs directed at me. [Triggers that are] sexually or racially oriented ... aren't as active on my radar. They're not an immediate and regular part of my lived experience, and it's important for me to make the effort to remain mindful of that." Bradford pauses, then continues. "Of course, some things are traumatic for all of us. And then there's if you've had trauma x, y, or z, those things might trigger you and not someone else. If you tried to block all triggering content [on social media], we would be looking at a giant, muted, blurred block for all of our investigative images."

The fact that digital content quickly traverses geographic boundaries means that a surprisingly large number of people can be emotionally affected by it. For example, the shock over George Floyd's killing expanded beyond communities in the United States to those overseas. Adebayo Okeowo, for example, is Nigerian and works for WITNESS, a nonprofit that trains activists how to capture civil and human rights violations on camera. He reflected on his reaction to the Floyd video: "As much as we know the police in Africa can be extreme … even we couldn't think of any cop who has done that, even though some have shot someone point blank. This was even more extreme [for them to do that] and even as cameras were rolling, as if that life didn't matter. People protested across the world, even in Nigeria, because that was such an unbelievable sight." Ultimately, the reaction to the images of Floyd's death strengthened activism on the continent. Okeowo said the fury over Floyd's killing and the ensuing uptick in the Black Lives Matter movement fed the Free Senegal protests and the #EndSARS police violence protests then raging in Africa.

> It would have still been an injustice if a white person had been killed that way, but it was more painful from a Black person's perspective because it seems to be a pattern: that disregard for a Black life. If I had been in South Africa I would have had a better sense of how the white community in South Africa responded, but I have a feeling that those who have been allies to the Black struggle would have responded like white allies in the US: with shock and disdain. … The anger was palpable in many parts of Africa because this was a Black person, the sense that this could happen to me. [People even started saying] maybe you shouldn't go to the U.S. because you could just be killed [for no reason], without any regard.

Like Clancy, who told the story of the white female protestor who threw her used tampon at her jailers when they refused to let her use the restroom, Okeowo uses an offline example to further explain the power of identity in reactions to upsetting events. He recalls an excursion he made with friends to an apartheid museum in Johannesburg. Two of the Black South Africans in his group refused to go in. "I remember it clearly. They couldn't go in and relive the horrors of the apartheid regime. They even questioned why there would be a museum set up to [display] imagery and facts about that [time]." Okeowo said he understands that there are important, valid reasons to preserve memory for those who have been victims as well as survivors and to share the horrors of history with those who did not experience that era first hand, but he also understands the visceral reaction of Black South Africans like his friends who have no desire to re-experience the trauma. While

Okeowo's example centers on images of atrocities featured in a physical museum, social media platforms have, in many instances, become those museums' digital equivalent.

Ultimately, our reactions to graphic images may differ based on age, gender, geography, race, or other demographics; they can also differ based on whether we've had similar previous experiences to those depicted or may have even been present for the event we are now watching unfold over digital space. They also differ based on our political persuasions; graphic images of aborted fetuses weaponized by the anti-choice movement in the United States will produce very different reactions depending on where one falls across the abortion divide, just as the attacks on the United States Capitol on January 6 will be seen either as heroic acts of patriotism or horrific acts of terrorism depending on whether one believes the disinformation President Trump spread about the integrity of the 2020 presidential election. How we feel about a photo of dead soldiers in Ukraine may radically differ depending on whether we are Russian or Ukrainian.

Author John Durham Peters has underscored the various ways in which witnessing violent events play out.[9] He has theorized that forms of witnessing reside on a continuum, ranging from being physically present at an event, to watching live transmission of the event (such as on a livestream), to visiting the historic site of an event or a museum exhibit about it, to experiencing a retelling of the event in a written, visual or audio format – with the types varying with the witnesses' proximity to the time and space of the underlying event. Each of these forms can mediate our responses, as in each scenario, our relationship to the material differs.

Michael Shaw addresses another kind of witnessing, a variant of retelling, one that takes the form of a media ritual. Memorials of major events in the media have become a regular part of the news stream. He said that the one-year, ten-year, and twenty-five-year time intervals have become standard prompts for major anniversary features, in which media organizations revisit violent attacks, devastating natural disasters, and other prominent cultural concussions. Framed as memorializing, the ensuing narrative, especially the imagery, is often re-traumatizing. In the case of 9/11, the graphic material paraded out by media organizations will reawaken painful memories, especially among those who most suffered through it. "Whether we are talking about 9/11 visuals of the planes hitting the towers or the famous image of the falling man, the rehash is often as emotionally toxic as it is gratuitous," Shaw said.

How we respond to graphic accounts varies not only with our own experiences but also with our immediate contexts. Our current emotional state, unrelated to the online content itself, can have a profound impact on our emotional response to that content: Did we recently give birth? Are we stuck at home with a screaming child? Are we at work? Are we alone in bed, late at night? In a crowded workplace,

---

[9] John Durham Peters, "Witnessing," 23 *Media Culture Society* 707 (2001) (discussed in Richardson 2020, 6).

surrounded by others? Staring down a final exam or other deadline? Unrelated stresses may prime us for a disproportionately strong or especially emotional response. Of course, our reactions may also be numbed or deadened. As Sontag explains, "For photographs to accuse ... they must shock. [But] shock can become familiar. Shock can wear off."[10] We can also be so distracted by immediate, everyday concerns that the impact of graphic content may not fully register. Our reactions are identity specific but also context contingent.

Shaw shared several examples in which the context of living and working in a pandemic drastically affected peoples' reactions to visual media and their work with that media. Threatened by isolation, the loss of routine, or the fear of getting sick and left to fend for oneself, the pandemic upended the assuredness of some of the most skilled practitioners.

After losing a close family member to COVID, an academic he worked with – someone well versed in analyzing documentary imagery – could no longer work with imagery at all. "COVID completely broke down this person's defenses," said Shaw. "It was really kind of stunning. It wasn't just 'I need some distance.' It was 'I can't do this anymore.'"

Given this variation in what people find upsetting, and when they find it upsetting, how might we approach graphic media content more thoughtfully, with an eye to minimizing the negative effects? Everything mentioned above suggests the need to be flexible with ourselves and others, to recognize that our reactions can change, and sometimes rapidly. As discussed in greater detail in Chapter 4, we need to give ourselves and others opportunities to choose how and when we engage with graphic content, which can have a dramatic effect on our well-being.

IDENTITY AS A PROTECTIVE FORCE

Our unique identities don't just make us vulnerable, however. They can also be our greatest strength.

As with our student who investigated atrocities in Iran, identity can be harnessed in ways that support resilience, such as when it helps us draw meaning from our act of witnessing trauma. Scott, the woman who worked at YouTube in content moderation, explained how her identity as a white woman and as a team manager may have helped to protect her from some of the worst emotional reactions to the difficult content she and her team processed. "With the privileges that my identity affords

---

[10] Sontag, *Regarding the Pain of Others*, 81–82. Sontag has also explained that it can be a good thing when people don't have an emotional reaction to every piece of content they encounter. As Sontag has warned, "it is not necessarily better to be moved. Sentimentality, notoriously, is entirely compatible with a taste for brutality and worse. ... People don't become inured to what they are shown ... because of the quantity of images dumped on them. It is passivity that dulls feeling. The states descriptive as apathy, moral or emotional anesthesia are full of feelings; the feelings are rage and frustration." Ibid. at 102.

me, I maybe had more agency than others," said Scott – agency that would give her a degree of relative freedom to set the terms of her engagement with the material. As we know, that agency, that sense of control, can work as a protective force.

Meg Satterthwaite, a clinical professor of law at New York University who has conducted extensive research into the psychosocial impacts of human rights work, emphasized the importance of adopting a holistic approach to thinking about identity and our reactions to difficult material, including how mindfulness of the potential impact that specific kinds of content can have on us can help ensure that the triggers we experience are processed in a way that supports well-being. She noted the importance of "reminding yourself that you're a human being and that part of you is being triggered all the time, whether you know it or not." Acknowledging those triggers is important in order to not become numb to imagery and thus the cruelties of the world. "If you're not aware of it there could be a callousness that's building up over time."

Satterthwaite praised the work of Arianna Schindel, an activist social worker based in New York who has supported a range of survivors of various forms of trauma and abuse, from domestic workers in the United States to LGBTQ+ activists in Uganda. Schindel created and runs a program called "Fire That Fuels." The program focuses on how to connect with the internal fire that energizes versus the fire that burns you – and the importance of recognizing that the source is often the same. When we are fueled to make change, we have a greater sense of control than when we passively absorb horrific news. Ultimately, this helps us to stave off the anxiety and depression that could develop.

Of course, not all of us are fueled or burned by the same material. Satterthwaite also emphasized how important it is for all of us to be thoughtful and deliberate in what material we share, taking into consideration other peoples' identities and the fact that they may have very different reactions to the material than we do: What one person finds inspiring and empowering may leave another shaken. "[We need to] meaningfully curate, not mindlessly forward stuff to people. Also not tag victims on Twitter. I'm thinking of the USA gymnastics team [and the lawsuit against Larry Nasser for chronic sexual abuse of young, female gymnasts]: I saw a Tweet from one of the elite gymnasts that said, 'Please stop tagging me on every Tweet about Larry Nasser.' It can be so retraumatizing for people. And for racist police violence, white people in particular need to be more aware about the impact of forwarding and linking [online content] in ways that make people click [on things] that they're not prepared to see."

Satterthwaite also stressed the need to move beyond trigger warnings that presuppose how certain groups may react to content and to give people explicit information that empowers people to make their own assessments. "The earlier trigger warnings we got were very much about who we *are* ('if you're a sexual violence victim, you may want to take care') versus what we'll *see* ('This contains images of X'). The latter seems so much more important." Ultimately, the more nuanced we are in telling what something we're sharing contains, the more viewers can prepare themselves for processing the material and adopt whatever protections they need to avoid being scalded.

Michael Shaw's work in visual media – specifically investigating how visual information impacts individuals and communities – is fueled by an experience that might have harmed him. He told us in an interview that his mother had been an artist who traveled in elite circles in the creative world. When Shaw was young, she had a mental breakdown, sometimes slipping into psychosis. Rather than fearing her, "I got good at decoding her language: I had [developed] an empathic connection with a creative person who, at the time, became overly dependent on visual language and the safety of metaphor. From that experience, I found greater significance in the visual world."

As a father, Shaw's interest in using visual information to relay information took another turn. He had become increasingly concerned about civic and political consciousness and wanted to find a way for his two young sons to access the news. So he created a cartoon called "Bag News" designed to render the day's *New York Times* top story in a picture sketched on a lunch bag. "My goal was to capture the facts and personalities [in the story] in this one cartoon. It was kind of compulsive. I did it every single weekday for 12 or 13 years." In 2004, this effort led him online to the blogosphere and the analysis of news images. It was a unique period of transition in which "the media lost exclusive control" over the dissemination of news and images, with politicians, political organizations, and corporations suddenly able to [bypass established media channels and] and go direct to the consumer." He has spent the last couple of decades examining news and images for meaning, trends, context, and fairness, to impart that appreciation to news consumers and media professionals.

NOT LOOKING AS A PROTECTIVE FORCE

Finally, when identity and well-being are at issue, "not looking" can sometimes be a powerful choice and a protective force. While millions of people may have mindlessly – or mindfully – watched footage of the George Floyd video, for example, an untold number of those who regularly work with graphic content chose not to look, despite their deep dedication to social justice and despite their regular exposure to videos of atrocities. Their reasons varied.

Elena Martin had just graduated from UC Berkeley when George Floyd was murdered and the footage hit her newsfeed. Like Haley Willis, Martin had worked with the Human Rights Center's Investigations Lab and was no stranger to graphic content. In fact, she had spent the last three years finding and corroborating graphic imagery related to conflicts and protests in Syria and Hong Kong.

"I was aware of [the video] as soon as it started spreading, that a man had been killed and it had been recorded," said Martin. "As soon as I saw that it was graphic content, I decided not to watch it. It felt very disrespectful to watch when it could be commodified and commercialized. ... As someone who was just a viewer, I didn't think it was my [place] to watch this. Also, I wouldn't want to have someone watch me suffer."

Liz Scott responded similarly when asked about the video of George Floyd's killing. "I didn't watch it. I try not to watch that kind of thing. I find it sad. As a society, we have an appetite for seeing Black and brown bodies have violence [perpetrated] against them. During the Arab Spring, we had this whole thing, people just so comfortable watching [the violence]." She paused. "In America, I don't know if it's similar but, as a white person seeing responses to videos of attacks [in Europe people say] 'We need to take this down' and the whole human rights [conversation about how this content should stay up for social justice reasons] is just *done*," she said, emphasizing the word "done" with a wave of her hand. "I just wish we could move beyond this desperation to share these videos that are so traumatizing. If you are already like, 'I need to rise up and end white supremacy in this country' then [you] don't need to watch that video. Especially when a journalist can watch it and do a write up or find another way to share that information."

At UC Berkeley School of Law, students have flocked to a two-unit course created and taught by Mallika Kaur, a Berkeley Law instructor and human rights lawyer, that focuses on understanding and strengthening responses to trauma and burnout in the profession. Kaur emphasizes to her students that "personal wiring matters" and that it's not a sign of weakness or defeat to not watch something. She said that what interacts with our personal identities and experiences and therefore triggers us can easily shift and so awareness is key. "One size doesn't fit all and that size changes over time," she said. Kaur didn't watch the George Floyd video herself because, she said, "I have watched enough graphic videos for a lifetime." Her students were ultimately split between those who had seen the video and those who chose not to look. Not looking at graphic imagery is a choice Kaur wholeheartedly endorses and one that is beginning to prevail among younger people seeking to be more thoughtful about what they consume online, she said. A prevalent response among many of her students was that people of color may especially not want to watch the video of George Floyd's killing and that not watching might be the best approach for them, but that it was especially important for white people to watch.

Often, people feel that they *have* to look at challenging videos or posts. For those who have a deep dedication to social justice, they may look to express solidarity or to connect with a national or international movement. But as our interviewees repeatedly underscored, if you're already aware of how people like those depicted in a photo or video are being treated in the broader society, there may be little additive value in looking at that photo or video and a relatively high potential for distress.

AWARENESS AS A PROTECTIVE FORCE

The imperative to understand how our unique identities make us both more vulnerable and more resilient to traumatic content leads us to one of the most critical and perhaps obvious ways we can maintain our health and well-being in the face of the world's traumatic events and conditions: by fostering greater awareness of ourselves and our reactions.

Studies on responses to trauma – including Satterthwaite et al's "A Culture of Unwellness,"[11] Dubberley et al's "Making Secondary Trauma a Primary Issue,"[12] and Baker et al's "Safer Viewing"[13] – note the importance of being aware of one's vulnerabilities and also of what constitutes vicarious trauma or burnout. Without cultivating this awareness, people can be left to suffer the effects: feeling distance from loved ones, irritability, reclusiveness, restlessness, depression, and more.

For "A Culture of Unwellness," Satterthwaite interviewed Alexa, who stressed the importance of awareness related to identity:

> I think on [the] awareness side, what we've tried to instill in the [Berkeley team] is that what's going to impact you is different from what impacts other people. So for some people it's seeing children killed. For others it may be beheadings. You don't know until you're in the material. So even in terms of the division of labor – to make sure you're not exposed to the stuff that's particularly challenging [for you] but for someone else who it doesn't affect as much can take that on. ... But also making sure that you're aware that what affects you may change not only between people but within yourself from day to day, depending on what your context is and what you're going through in your personal life. So there may be times when, in our own personal lives, when we may be more vulnerable and really don't have the resources and reserves to deal with the trauma and that might be a point in time when it's good to take a break.[14]

What does cultivating awareness look like? What it doesn't look like is attending a one-off talk from a mental health expert who exhorts us to be aware of ourselves and colleagues. It takes sustained attention to – and an ability to repeatedly check in with – ourselves to know what works for us individually in terms of reducing distress, what works for our friends and colleagues, and what does not.

In the Human Rights Center's Investigations Lab, students would often start the semester taking stock: What is normal *for me?* How much do I sleep when I'm feeling healthy and balanced? How much do I exercise? What foods do I normally eat? Identifying this baseline and having awareness of what's normal or optimal for us (something that changes over time) is essential to being able to identify if something shifts within us.

---

[11] Margaret Satterthwaite, Sarah Knuckey, Ria Singh Sawhney, Katie Wightman, Rohini Bagrodia, and Adam Brown, "From a Culture of Unwellness to Sustainable Advocacy: Organizational Responses to Mental Health Risks in the Human Rights Field," 28 *Review of Law and Social Justice* 443 (2018).

[12] Sam Dubberley, Elizabeth Griffin, and Haluk Mert Bal, "Making Secondary Trauma a Primary Issue: A Study of Eyewitness Media and Vicarious Trauma on the Digital Frontlines," *First Draft* (2015).

[13] Elise Baker, Eric Stover, Rohini Haar, Andrea Lampros, and Alexa Koenig, "Safer Viewing: A Study of Secondary Trauma Mitigation Techniques in Open Source Investigations," 22 *Health and Human Rights Journal* 293 (2020).

[14] Satterthwaite et al, "Culture of Unwellness," at 530.

As the *New York Times*' Haley Willis recounted in the introduction, her response to traumatic imagery while working in the Investigations Lab as a student was, at first, to sleep a lot. She didn't realize that this was a trauma response until she realized that sleeping so much wasn't normal for her.

This awareness of self has to transfer to an awareness of others if we are to protect ourselves, our families, and our colleagues. Mindlessly sharing traumatic imagery or hateful content without an awareness of another person's vulnerabilities can be similarly problematic. As several content moderators told us: Don't just share troubling content because *you think* it will somehow educate people. What affects you may not affect someone else in the same way, and vice versa.

Ultimately, what came through in the interviews and from our research is that it's better to be thoughtful about whether or not to watch a video than to do so reflexively, or to do so *because* we identify with the content. One of the most salient considerations is whether some graphic content might be more palatable if consumed through news gathering sources that provide context and analysis. There is inestimable value in high-quality journalism. Professional media organizations may package an incident in a way that communicates the underlying facts without the same level of toxicity and immediacy of a single, unedited video, which can leave a viewer feeling raw.

Our hope is that awareness of the harms of the world can lead to empowerment and help people mobilize to contribute to positive change. Rawness or depression rarely results in productive action. The goal is to be able to engage with this kind of content as needed over the long haul, without adding to layers of trauma that may have already accumulated. Journalistic reporting – which rarely if ever relies on a single photo or video, but usually pulls together multiple human perspectives – may also tell a more complete story than a single video or photo ever could, challenging the misinformation that we know is prevalent online and weaving in the critical context that helps us place a person's story in the world.

4

Agency and Control

The founders of Open Source Researchers of Color (OSROC) are digital natives, people who have come of age at a time when the Internet, smart phones, and other connected technologies have largely replaced our analog ways. They're also mostly twenty-somethings who have immersed themselves in the digital documentation of human rights violations, poring over videos and photographs from war zones in order to shed light on potential war crimes. In short, they've got skills and awareness to share with the rest of us about how to handle graphic, traumatic material day in and out.

"I really needed to do [investigative] work in crowded environments, not alone, not late at night, not in my room. The big [thing that has helped] is separation of space, being intentional about space and time. I don't scroll in bed, I don't read the news late at night," said OSROC co-founder Rachael Cornejo, who works in cybersecurity, explaining how she protected herself when working on a series of social media videos posted by ISIS and other terrorist groups. When suspecting she may be confronted with distressing material, she minimizes the screen size and turns down the volume or shuts off the sound while preparing herself for what she is about to see.

"I'm [now] more intentional about how I use my phone and my screen time," said Elena Martin, an IT security practitioner, explaining how her professional training has influenced her sense of self-efficacy, including how she chooses to use digital tools in her personal life.

The strategies Cornejo and Martin employ to maximize their agency over distressing material in order to minimize the risk of harm are supported by science.

Dr. Metin Başoğlu, former director and founder of the Section of Trauma Studies at King's College London's Institute of Psychiatry, as well as founder of the Istanbul Center for Behavior Research and Therapy in Turkey, has worked with thousands of survivors of atrocity, exploring effective treatment for those who are struggling in the aftermath of war, torture, domestic violence, and natural disasters. He and his partner, Dr. Ebru Şalcıoğlu, have collaborated with other researchers to explore whether PTSD treatments can be made incredibly efficient so as to treat the maximum possible number of those affected by mass traumatic events, considering that victims may number into the thousands, and also find ways to better prepare people for mass atrocities before they occur in order to stave off PTSD.[1]

Many of the treatments Basoglu and Salciaglu have pioneered are built off the insight that PTSD/PTSI can manifest in a number of ways, including as anxiety and depression. According to Basoglu and Salciaglu, anxiety stems from having a perceived lack of personal control over a situation, while depression stems from a lack of hope. Thus, these two phenomena can be countered by helping individuals maximize their sense of control and strengthening their hope for a better future.[2] Such insights may help all of us think through how anxiety and depression might be staved off when confronting challenging information online.

Even without awareness of Basoglu's theory, many of those we interviewed spoke of the protective effects of increasing control over disturbing online content by exercising personal agency over their interaction with social media – something that the pioneering digital documenter and activist Eileen Clancy has lauded as "a protective force." Gabi Ivens of Human Rights Watch, who works with distressing visual content almost daily, underscored the value of increasing "control" over one's interaction with the content by having set protocols for when and how one looks at graphic imagery, while Keramet Reiter, a professor at UC Irvine who researches the effects of solitary confinement, commented that "the worst thing in the world is to feel totally helpless."

Across the board, interviewees emphasized that one of the most powerful ways to exercise agency is to increase awareness of the effects of shifting when, where, and how one accesses and uses social media and other sources of distressing imagery – and then using those insights to minimize the risks that come with online engagement.

According to experts, the risk of harm can be mitigated by biological, psychological, social, and environmental interventions. Biological approaches include focusing on what you were born with, such as various personality and temperamental traits. Psychological approaches focus on working with your emotional and cognitive attributes, such as your sense of humor and your perceptions of self. Social approaches include refining things like your interpersonal skills and relationships, including enhancing social support. Finally, environmental approaches focus on phenomena that are external to you but provide context around you, such as your socioeconomic status or various life events.[3]

---

[1] See, for example, Metin Başoğlu, Maria Livanou, and Ebru Şalcıoğlu, "A Single Session with an Earthquake Simulator for Traumatic Stress in Earthquake Survivors," 160 *American Journal of Psychiatry* 788–790 (2003).

[2] Metin Başoğlu, *Torture and Its Definition in International Law: An Interdisciplinary Approach* (Oxford University Press 2017).

[3] Carl C. Bell, "Exposure to a Traumatic Event Does Not Automatically Put a Person on a Path to Develop PTSD: The Importance of Protective Factors to Promote Resiliency," Gift from within-PTSD Resources for Survivors and Caregivers, available at: www.giftfromwithin.org/html/promote.html#8back.

As a starting place and as previously discussed, it's important to recognize that while a significant percentage of people will experience a traumatic event during their lifetime – nearly 60 percent of men and 50 percent of women in the United States alone[4] – traumatic stress does not automatically cause PTSI.[5] Instead, most people who are affected by a traumatic event will adapt within three to six months.[6] In addition, according to researchers CC Bell and H Suggs, "repeated exposure to minimal or moderate stressors can build resilience,"[7] as does increasing individuals' sense of self-efficacy and exercising power over their actions and their lives.[8]

Michael Elsanadi, one of the founders of OSROC who worked as an investigator analyzing social media content of atrocities in Syria for the human rights nonprofit Mnemonic, paused as he thought about his own strategies. "A major tip I'd give is to slow down. There's always outraged people saying 'How are people not talking about this?!?' Don't give in [to that]. There are always people talking about things. I find that slowing down my news consumption, [reading full, in-depth articles] as opposed to just looking at the headlines, I feel better about what [I'm looking at] because I have more context." Similarly, Martin explained, "I find it more insightful to read through a document I'm interested in as opposed to reading a series of headlines and being overwhelmed with the amount of information we receive on a daily basis."

Such protective measures as slowing down can also help with preventing shock from seeing something you're emotionally unprepared to see, which is probably the most cited source of harm when dealing with emotional online material. Researchers and practitioners have repeatedly found that when people are surprised by graphic or emotionally distressing content, they are more often disturbed by it. They may

---

4 National Center for PTSD, "How Common Is PTSD in Adults?," U.S. Department of Veterans Affairs.

5 While most people don't develop PTSD from a single event, the number of people who will experience PTSD during their lifetime is notable: in the United States, that equates to approximately 8 percent of women and 4 percent of men, with approximately 12 million people in the U.S. suffering from PTSD at any given time. National Center for PTSD, "How Common Is PTSD in Adults?," U.S. Department of Veterans Affairs.

6 D. S. Riggs, B. O. Rothbaum, and E. B. Foa, "A Prospective Examination of Symptoms of Posttraumatic Stress Disorder in Victims of Nonsexual Assault," 10 *Journal of Interpersonal Violence* 201–214 (1995), cited in Carl C. Bell, "Exposure to a Traumatic Event Does Not Automatically Put a Person on a Path to Develop PTSD: The Importance of Protective Factors to Promote Resiliency," Gift from within-PTSD Resources for Survivors and Caregivers, available at: www.giftfromwithin.org/html/promote.html#8back.

7 Carl C. Bell, "Exposure to a Traumatic Event Does Not Automatically Put a Person on a Path to Develop PTSD: The Importance of Protective Factors to Promote Resiliency," Gift From Within-PTSD Resources for Survivors and Caregivers, available at: www.giftfromwithin.org/html/promote.html (last visited July 12, 2022) (citing C. C. Bell and H. Suggs, "Using Sports to Strengthen Resiliency in Children-Training Heart: Using Sports to Create Resiliency, Child and Adolescent Psychiatric Clinics of North America," 7 *Child and Adolescent Psychiatric Clinics of North America* 859–865 (1998)).

8 C. Regehr, J. Hill, T. Knott, and B. Sault, "Social Support, Self-efficacy and Trauma in New Recruits and Experienced Firefighters," 19 *Stress and Health* 189 (2003) (as cited in C.C. Bell).

later find the images interfere with their thoughts, their quality of sleep, or other aspects of well-being.[9] Gabi Ivens of Human Rights Watch spoke about her strategy for minimizing unwelcome surprises: "Now, when I'm potentially going to see something graphic or distressing, I ask people to tell me exactly what I'm going to see [before I view it]." Sam Dubberley, who has trained teams of students from around the world to comb social media for evidence of atrocities for Amnesty International, explains that having that kind of advance notice helps you prepare mentally and make an informed decision about the right time and place to view a video or photograph or social media post – or whether you want to see the content at all.

Trigger warnings on both social media and even twenty-four-hour cable news networks are becoming increasingly common – and welcomed. When we spoke to Ariel Newman, she was a 19-year-old student at Sonoma State University in northern California who spent much of the pandemic in remote classes. She got her first cell phone in sixth grade but didn't have access to the Internet for social media. She texted with the few friends who had phones at her small private school. Newman said she was always sensitive to images in social media, which led her to protest in the wake of George Floyd's murder and has also led her to be protective about what she views. "I think there should be a trigger warning, if it's graphic or upsetting. Maybe the trigger warning should include a description," suggested Newman, who says any story about child molestation really unsettles her, and that it is important to know the particulars of what she may be viewing. "I am very sensitive, and if I see something scary in a movie, I won't be able to sleep all night. If I see a trigger warning, I think about what kind of space I am in. Am I in a space to handle it? If I feel like I can, I will."

Agency can also be maximized with what one *does* with one's social media engagement. NYU researcher Meg Satterthwaite explains, "If you can find some way to reconnect, take action and have an efficacy in the world and can make things better, that helps. It might be a small piece of research that leads to a change like an indictment [at the International Criminal Court]. If you can find some way to act out, that restores your sense of agency."

Of course, not everyone can, will, or even should send information they find upsetting to the International Criminal Court or have any concrete way of making large-scale impact on a distressing global event. But everyone can think critically about their own agency, and whether they can do something with what they've learned, such as reaching out to a legislator or a reliable news agency, making a donation to a nonprofit that works on a related issue, or informing a friend.

The urge to be proactive with distressing online information may be instinctive, explaining much of the compulsion to forward or repost upsetting material. Focusing on the meaning behind your engagement (as discussed in Chapter 6) and how that engagement potentially contributes to a greater good, can be a powerful way to tilt the balance away from feeling depleted and toward feeling empowered.

---

[9] Margaret Satterthwaite et al, "From a 'Culture of Unwellness."

Sometimes, drawing *more* on tech can help. Several professionals we interviewed who analyze distressing content talked about turning their screen to grayscale so that images would be rendered in black and white instead of in color and thus appear less jarring. Others spoke of slowing down or speeding up playback when watching a video to lessen the emotional resonance. YouTube has made this process incredibly easy by including an ability to shift playback speed right from the video interface.

Ashley Bradford, the technologist mentioned earlier, is creating software designed to help investigators with resiliency when viewing graphic content. He explains that tweaking how you interact with a video can have a huge protective effect. In 2020 and early 2021, he worked with a team of UC Berkeley students to create a tool that uses object detection – a form of artificial intelligence – to automatically identify and blur especially graphic material. He hopes this may help war crimes investigators, for example, by automatically detecting blood or beheadings before human eyes stumble across such content, and flagging or blurring the content before humans view the atrocity and shock sets in. The blurring can be easily turned off, however, if an investigator needs that detail.

> Such technology puts greater control in the hands of the user. By contrast, tech tools like autoplay, which enables videos to automatically play as you come across them in your feed, robs viewers of control over what they see. Human rights investigators often advise their teams to turn off autoplay on social media feeds when that functionality is available. In *Bearing Witness While Black*, Allissa Richardson quotes sociologist Eve Ewing on this issue: "I've been very vocal about pushing news media outlets to not have autoplay videos because there have been times … that I'm reading an article and then I scroll down and this video starts playing that I didn't consent to watching. … I used to know people that really made me feel like if I didn't watch videos of black people dying then I didn't care or that I was somehow sheltering myself from reality when in fact I think that we vastly underestimate the trauma that we endure by watching videos like that and also we overestimate the degree to which those videos actually make a difference [in terms of advancing social change]."[10]

Cornejo, who works in cybersecurity and was one of the people we interviewed who didn't watch the George Floyd videos, explained, "You don't need to see a video to believe it's real. Since I was already plugged into networks to respond, I didn't think I needed to put myself through this emotional reaction. It felt almost disrespectful to his family to watch it. How much do we need to rely on graphic content to motivate ourselves to take action? And how can we build a world where that's not the case?"

Keramet Reiter, the professor at the University of California, Irvine, who investigates the harms of solitary confinement, similarly struggled with whether to watch.

---

[10] Allissa Richardson, *Bearing Witness While Black: African Americans, Smartphones, and the New Protest #Journalism* (Oxford University Press 2020): 167.

Several of her students were upset that she hadn't seen the video. "I was teaching a criminology class, and I know bearing witness has value. But part of my outrage was, 'Why was anyone surprised?'" Like Reiter, several interviewees explained that they didn't need to watch the video to know that Black men, women, and children are killed in the United States at a rate disproportionate to others. These interviewees stressed the importance of knowing *why* you're watching a particularly upsetting piece of content, especially a video depicting something as intimate as a human being's last minutes. As Reiter asked, "How do I look, but look ethically in a way that isn't voyeuristic, and respects the voices that I heard?"

Haley Willis, who was part of the team that analyzed the footage of Floyd's murder and provided surrounding context for the *New York Times*' visual investigation, had no choice but to watch – and to watch over and over again. Instead, what she and her team grappled with was what to *show*, essentially what visuals to select for others to watch. "What is worth showing, what is exploitative?" She expressed gratitude that her boss, Whitney Hurst, assumed the important leadership work of helping to guide their team through thoughtful responses to those questions.

Hurst similarly struggled with how to approach the material. "On a personal level, of course, seeing it was horrifying.

> I mean, it's hard to even come up with the adjectives to describe what it's like to see that on a personal level. Also, I'm Black. And so it had personal resonance, and … I think a lot of Black people can see themselves in this kind of material. It can be traumatic on a bunch of different levels. This is not something new. Obviously, there's photographs of lynching and stuff, going back to the 1800s. But, you know, something at this level hadn't been so thoroughly documented. Obviously, this was a huge news story. The original police statements to the press didn't mention what we actually now know happened. … It seemed like a pretty clear-cut case, once [we] actually looked at the footage. And so I think we, as an investigation team, thought it was something important for us to do. And then [the video] had very quickly ricocheted around the Internet and become a big story. And we wanted to see if there was any sort of additional understanding of the events that we could bring to it. [T]his stuff is so complex, and there are no easy calls. And, you know, we had to go into all of these kinds of editorial decisions with a tremendous amount of humility, because you have to be open to maybe you don't get it right, or maybe some people in the country think that you didn't do the right thing. And I definitely thought about how it would be received by people of color, by anybody."
> Hurst also underscored the importance of returning control to the viewer. "If you don't want to watch, I think you should have the option. I don't think it should be like something auto playing on your … TV constantly or on your phone."

Gabi Ivens of Human Rights Watch has struggled with the blurred lines that the videos of George Floyd's murder created between her personal and professional online identities – identities she has worked hard to keep separate, largely as a form of self-protection. "You're working on those videos in your job, but you're also seeing them on your [personal] news sites, on your Instagram." She explained how difficult it was seeing the video on both work sites *and* personal sites. "When you see it in every part of your world. ... I think that's really tricky."

Sam Dubberley asked a question of us in return that tied the video of Floyd's murder to the issue of agency, underscoring the importance of knowing the meaning of why one is looking: "How do we use this content to create [a common sense of] humanity?" As he noted, the killing's location in the United States might help with motivating action domestically in ways that don't often occur with international tragedies. "We get outraged about things close to home like George Floyd, but not kids drowning in the Mediterranean." Hence the role of the video of Floyd's killing in expanding the Black Lives Matter movement.

While it can be important to engage with issues on social media without turning away, sometimes, as we've seen, turning away can itself be a powerful act of protective agency. Eileen Clancy illuminated for us several other "protective forces." She highlighted "analysis as a protective force," in which conducting an intellectual analysis of a video or other distressing type of content becomes a form of agency that can help dampen the potentially negative psychological effects of engaging with upsetting material. For example, she explained how analyzing videos of police overreach and sharing that imagery and her findings with journalists and lawyers helped her to process such content in a way that was likely emotionally protective.

Josiah Thompson, who discussed with us everything from his investigation into President John F. Kennedy's killing to the murder of six-year-old JonBenét Ramsey at her Colorado home in 1996, similarly referenced the analytical process as a potentially protective force. When reflecting on how he coped with the graphic material and why it didn't have more of a lasting negative impact, he emphasized that how and why you are engaging with the material matters. Like surgeons operating in order to save someone's life, exposing them to sights of internal anatomy at which others might recoil: "The point is that [in a forensic investigation] you're looking there to find something. I mean you're not just ... idly looking, you're there to determine something. One looks at the gory pictures in order to understand what happened." According to neuroscientists and psychologists, such analysis may be protective because it activates a different part of your brain than that which usually responds to trauma: the part that handles logic instead of emotion.

Michael Elsanadi touched on a related point, but instead of focusing on the protective role of the viewer's own analysis, he pointed to the power of watching an interpretation or analysis of a video, such as you might see in a news description of the video or event, as opposed to watching the footage of the event itself: "I think it's sometimes important for people to see graphic content to know what's happened [but] it doesn't have to be raw footage, it can be an analysis. [Watching a documentary] may be more productive than [allowing oneself to be] ... flooded with [original] information on news feeds."

The author Allissa Richardson has analogized today's videos of the killing of Black men to "lynching postcards," photographs that circulated widely in the late-nineteenth and early to mid-twentieth centuries. As with the photo of Peter and his scars mentioned in Chapter 1, those photographs were used by abolitionists to bear critical witness to the crimes and cruelties perpetrated during those eras. But the postcards also treated lynchings as a spectacle and were deployed by racists to reinforce white supremacist ideology. Like those photos, today's smartphone footage "also has the potential to toe the line between digital tyranny that upholds white supremacy and visual evidence that galvanizes change."[11]

This theme reverberates in Richardson's interview with Dread Scott, a visual artist especially known for his redesign of the official flag of the National Association for the Advancement of Colored People (NAACP). Videos that depict the killing of Black men, he tells her "have helped increasing numbers of people see the depth of the problem, but left to [their own they're] just going to be sort of like lynching photos,"[12] which were too often used to terrorize Black communities by amplifying Black deaths in ways that were highly voyeuristic. Thus, when one does not need to be convinced that an event happened, it may actually be most protective – and most respectful – to not look.

Laura van Dernoot Lipsky, an expert in minimizing the harms of trauma exposure, explained that navigating the line between watching and not watching is an important one: "You have to be very intentional about this exposure, to be really, really mindful about what you're exposed to in your life, particularly when exposure is optional." She underscored the importance of limiting one's viewing of news, including on social media, stressing that "there are other ways to bear witness." She emphasizes the importance of not just waking up and grabbing a portable device to see what's happening in the world but integrating intentionality into our engagement by being deliberate about when we scroll social media or watch the news. Similarly, Meg Satterthwaite underscored the importance of mindfulness around how, when and whether to engage, explaining that it's important to be thoughtful about when we go online, and not just "scroll through Twitter while eating our cereal in the morning."

A study led by UC Berkeley's Elise Baker called *Safer Viewing*, which we co-authored, looked at the specific tools and techniques student investigators use and what they feel works best when working with graphic imagery and trying to mitigate secondary trauma. While specifically evaluating the experiences of students who work with human rights–related content, the findings are consistent with other research and can serve as guideposts for a general audience. Six general practices came to the surface as potentially protective. These were (1) limiting exposure to graphic content, (2) "processing" graphic content by discussing it with others,

---

[11]   Ibid. at 168.
[12]   Ibid. at 166.

(3) drawing boundaries between one's personal life and online investigations, (4) bringing positivity into investigations, (5) learning from more experienced investigators, and (6) employing a combination of these techniques. The research team also advised institutions to train students on secondary trauma mitigation strategies, to properly label videos and photos as containing graphic content, in order to warn those who may come across it later, and to emphasize self-care in the work.[13]

Lili Siri Spira, Rachael Cornejo, and Pearlé Nwaezeigwe, the co-creators of the organization RatedR: Resistance, Resiliency, Revolution,[14] which provides suggestions for maximizing psychological well-being when handling graphic content, all transitioned to tech-based jobs immediately following their graduation from UC Berkeley. They started RatedR when they recognized the heightened need for people to implement self-care practices and address vicarious trauma in the "digital days" that encompassed the pandemic, the launch of the Black Lives Matter movement, heightened attention to sexual violence as part of the #metoo and #timesup movements, and global uprisings in response to spreading authoritarianism. The site now offers a series of toolkits for those most affected by trauma and their allies to strengthen their self-care and resiliency.

In a 2021 talk that Spira and Cornejo gave to the Diana Initiative, they discussed how they had adopted a sensitivity to the potential for trauma and secondary trauma in online engagement and the importance of building resiliency to that potential while working in open-source investigations and cybersecurity at UC Berkeley. Once they left the university and started working in tech, they recognized that all people who engage with digital content could benefit from building resilience to help stave off the potential negative consequences of difficult material they might encounter online.[15]

Many of us keep waiting for the news to become net positive, something that's unlikely to happen and over which we have little control. However, even if we can't always control what we are exposed to, we can control how we engage with it, and that in turn, can contribute to an eventual net plus. As Emily and Amelia Nagoski, authors of the book *Burnout: The Secret to Unlocking the Stress Cycle* write, "[Y]ou don't have to wait for the world to be better before you make your life better – and by making your life better, you make the world better."[16]

For those who aren't engaging with graphic imagery for work but may stumble across it in their everyday lives, these strategies – and a handful of others – ultimately translate into the "tips and tricks," below.

---

[13] E. Baker, E. Stover, R. Haar, A. Lampros, and A. Koenig, "Safer Viewing: A Study of Secondary Trauma Mitigation Techniques in Open Source Investigations," 22 *Health and Human Rights* 293 (2020).

[14] "RatedR: Resistance. Revolution. Resilience Website," available at: www.RatedResilient.com.

[15] Rachael Cornejo and Lili Siri Spira, "Beyond Burnout: Hacking Your Way to a Healthier Work-Life Balance," The Diana Initiative, available at: www.youtube.com/watch?v=ypWMGr2u6SE (last visited July 14, 2022).

[16] Nagoski and Nagoski, *Burnout*, 215.

"TIPS AND TRICKS"

All of the following strategies are designed to increase the viewer's agency and control and thus minimize the likelihood of anxiety triggered by repeat exposure to potentially upsetting material:

Make sure you are as healthy physically as you can be before you look: Have you recently showered, eaten, drunk water, slept? As emphasized by the founders of RatedR, whenever engaging with potentially difficult or upsetting material, it's important to start with a solid foundation of "food, water, and sleep." When tired, hungry, or thirsty, you may find yourself emotionally raw and thus especially easy to trigger. Once your body is at a healthy baseline, you can begin building your resiliency strategy.

Mind *what* you eat and drink: Of course, not all food and drink is equally helpful. Mariana Jones,[17] who has worked for YouTube's Trust and Safety team, recalled that a therapist in her office once saw her pouring herself a huge cup of coffee. The therapist exclaimed, "What are you doing?" then explained how the coffee would soon be flooding her system with caffeine, when she was already in a hyperaroused state from the content she was viewing. What we ingest affects our reaction to the materials we encounter online and how equipped we are to process that material; water helps us biologically digest the material in a way that coffee won't. Many digital investigators we talked with (and with whom we've worked) will regularly remind each other to "drink water" when heading down the rabbit hole of online content.

Have a reason to look or watch: As explained above and as underscored by Eileen Clancy and Josiah Thompson, having a specific reason to look at a graphic video or photograph and having a task affiliated with that viewing can be protective. If you don't have a specific reason for watching, consider whether you can get information about the incident in some other way, including through a medium that may not be as emotive or graphic as video, such as a newspaper article.

Turn off the sound the first time you watch a potentially disturbing video: The most upsetting content associated with a video is often the audio: the child screaming for its parent, the woman begging for her life, the man crying out for his mother, or the person spewing racist, misogynistic, or homophobic slurs. Turning the sound off (or way down) can soften the emotional impact.

Scroll through the thumbnails of a video and scan the comments that surround it to prepare yourself mentally for what you're about to see – and then decide if you really want to see it, now or ever. Is "now" the right time to watch? Are you about to go to bed? Should you wait until morning, so the images and sounds don't play on repeat in your head while you struggle to sleep, or disrupt your dreams?

[17] We use a pseudonym for Mariana throughout this book given the sensitive nature of what she revealed.

Limit where you watch upsetting material to keep negative memories from contaminating places you'd like to protect: Is "this" the place you want affiliated with that potentially distressing material? Or is there another place where you should watch this? Not all of us have the luxury of options for where we view online content. However, for those who do, it can be helpful to create a space where you engage with upsetting social media. It's especially helpful to keep digital devices and the watching of distressing or graphic content out of your bedroom. If you live in a studio apartment, then dedicating a space for scrolling on social media (other than your bed!) can help.

Develop a ritual before and after looking at distressing content: In addition to separating where you look at social media from other personal space, develop a routine before you begin to scroll through the news. This could be taking five deep breaths or rolling your shoulders back or clearing your workspace. As importantly, leave the session on your computer or phone with a little ritual. This could mean intentionally closing the laptop or placing the phone in another room or repeating a transition statement out loud, such as: "Moving on." Ultimately, as Spira, Cornejo, and Nwaezeigwe of RatedR explain: "Wellness is not a state of being but a state of *action*. It is the freedom to move fluidly through the cyclical, oscillating experiences of being human."[18] Rituals can help us transition through those cycles.

Minimize the screen size: If you know you're going to watch something upsetting, minimizing the video size can lessen the impact. Is there any practical reason why you need to see someone killed on a large screen? Or can you get the gist and enough of the detail from viewing something smaller?

Block disturbing imagery if you need to look at the material repeatedly or for long periods: If engaging with the material for school or work and you need to view the material repeatedly for analytical purposes, you can place a post-it or piece of paper over the distressing image(s) if not necessary to your immediate task. Many analysts, war crimes investigators, and others will block the graphic details of a killing or other atrocity while scrutinizing the detail in the surroundings for clues regarding where or when the crime took place, for example.

Give your body a break: After you've viewed upsetting material on your computer, tablet, or phone, whether for minutes or hours, it can help to move in order to process what you've experienced. *Burnout* authors Emily and Amelia Nagoski explain how our body needs to metabolize its experiences and find a way to release the trauma we've ingested. They argue that people need to "complete" a biological stress cycle through physical activity in order to minimize any mental exhaustion or overwhelm. Walking a dog, going for a run, taking a yoga class, blasting music, and having a one-minute solo "dance party," can all be ways to physically "metabolize" the stressful material to which you've been exposed.

---

[18] Emily Nagoski and Amelia Nagoski, *Burnout: The Secret to Unlocking the Stress Cycle* (Ballantine Books 2019): 215.

Do something with what you've learned: As noted earlier in this chapter, depression has been linked to a lack of hope and anxiety to a lack of control. Taking concrete action based on what you've seen can provide a sense of hope that change can happen, and with it, can help protect you from feeling helpless. This could mean raising funds to support those who've been hurt; protesting an injustice; organizing a conversation to discuss and debate critical social issues; writing to legislators or others in power to influence their actions; and taking small steps to change your own behavior, if potentially part of the problem.

Finally, once you've finished viewing upsetting online material, consider reaching out to others in order to find comfort in being surrounded by supportive human beings, to discuss what you've seen, or to brainstorm what action you might take if next steps aren't clear. As we discuss in Chapter 5, building a community with whom you can share your reactions – especially in person – is yet another way to protect yourself from harm and put what you've learned to positive use.

5

Community as a Protective Force

Our student team's task in the Investigations Lab seemed simple enough and not particularly graphic in nature: comb Twitter to find harassment, disinformation, and politically divisive information directed against immigrants en route from Mexico to the United States. It was fall 2019, at the height of the Trump Administration's vitriol against immigrants, and on the heels of migrant caravans arriving at the US border and unaccompanied children being kept in cages. Trump's strategies to deter undocumented immigrants involved separating thousands of children from their parents, deporting or jailing parents, and holding children in substandard conditions, without regular access to "showers, clean clothes, toothbrushes or proper beds."[1]

After a few weeks of work on the project, the note that popped up on Andrea's Slack channel from Maria di Franco, the student team leader, said simply: "It's affecting us. Can we meet?"

The "it" di Franco referred to was the barrage of hateful language – "insects," "rats," "invasion," "dirty," "rapists," and worse – that had surfaced in social media posts, referencing immigrants. The racist words and sentiments were not new, of course, just renewed, recycled, and regurgitated for the latest wave of xenophobia. But in this round of anti-immigrant hate, the main channel for spreading the online vitriol – social media – was easier to access, faster, and more virulent than the channels that were used in our analog past. This content was also amplified on news channels, such as Fox.

The students had been assigned to work with Brandie Nonnecke, the co-founder and director of UC Berkeley's CITRIS Policy Lab at the Center for Information Technology Research. Nonnecke was researching the trajectory of hate-filled harassment, disinformation, and other politically divisive language on Twitter and she wanted the students to take a deep dive to document the trends and swim to wherever the language led.

---

[1] "Kids in Cages: Inhumane Treatment at the Border: Testimony of Clara Long Before the U.S. House Committee on Oversight and Reform, Subcommittee on Civil Rights and Civil Liberties," Human Rights Watch, July 11, 2019.

The students, mostly eighteen- to twenty-two-year-olds, scoured the Internet from their cramped dorm rooms, coffee shops, or the Human Rights Center house on the UC Berkeley campus. They found and meticulously added racist, misleading, and otherwise hateful posts to a spreadsheet, day after day, week after week. As the semester waned, the preponderance of hate felt like too much.

While all of the student researchers had been through "resiliency training" to learn tools and techniques to guard against the worst effects of viewing graphic or otherwise upsetting content, they needed something more to cope with what they were feeling – and immediately. They assembled one evening in the Human Rights Center's seminar room: five students, one undergraduate team leader, one graduate student, and Andrea. They ordered pizzas, kept the lights low, and started with a check-in on how the work was affecting them.

One student said it was making her feel cynical about humanity. Another said it felt like a personal attack and was making her sad and scared. And another said it was making her angry at everyone, even her beloved housemates, for not understanding.

The students went around the table to express their reactions to the content they had been marinating in over the past many weeks. "Now that you've shared your feelings," Andrea asked, "what do we actually know to be true about immigrants?" The student investigators took turns sharing positive words and phrases and telling stories about people in their families and communities. Some students were immigrants themselves or the children of immigrants. Gisela Perez de Acha Chavez, a Mexican journalist who worked with the team as a graduate student instructor, taught everyone a song/prayer from her *abuela*. Those gathered sang it together.

Others offered words like: "hardworking," "courageous," "kind," "my father," "my mother," "promise," "enrich," "culture," and more. The group wrote the words with colored markers on a piece of butcher paper in the center of the table. In community, the group enveloped themselves in positive words and images to push away the violent, often racist words used to depict those who immigrated to the United States.

Did this evening help students override the negative emotions they experienced while documenting hate? Not entirely. But the exercise strengthened a key tool we all have to mitigate secondary trauma caused by difficult content – whether we're researchers on the frontlines immersed in visual depictions of violence day in and day out, or occasional viewers – an expression of collective grief and community support.

The students, in this case, had analytically processed the content leading up to and reflective of Trump's policies – the patterns and use of xenophobia and racism, the history of anti-immigrant policies, and more. But they had not yet met to do one simple but powerful thing: express their sadness, grief, and anger about this cruel treatment of fellow humans.

In *Kitchen Table Wisdom: Stories that Heal*, Dr. Rachel Naomi Remen says (as noted in the opening to *Graphic*) that it's impossible to be "immersed in suffering and loss daily and not be touched by it."[2] She explains how the ability to deal with trauma and loss is fundamental to our ability to truly be present in our daily lives. We distance ourselves from the pain to protect ourselves, but ultimately that distancing from pain distances us from life. She says we're adversely affected "not because we don't care but because we don't grieve."

What exactly are we grieving? That depends on what we've lost. The loss may be one of hope, of optimism, of a belief in humanity's essential goodness, of a sense of safety. It may be a loss of innocence about the world and how it works, including who we are and how we fit in it. While we need to be realistic about violence and vengefulness in the world, that reality can be sad, disheartening, and a bitter pill to swallow.

How can we grieve? Our grieving can be singular, but it can also come from the collective processing of difficult experiences. Research and practice tell us that social support is essential to mitigating both primary and secondary trauma, as well as to other forms of health and wellness. Conversely, viewing and trying to process traumatic, hateful, or graphic content alone – a seemingly frequent state during the COVID-19 pandemic – can make us more vulnerable.

The father of positive psychology Martin E.P. Seligman has much to say about the power of relationships as a cornerstone of resilience. He offers the basic measurable elements of "well-being theory," which recognizes the power of positive emotions (which includes happiness and life satisfaction), engagement, connection, meaning, and achievement to overall wellness.[3] Many of these elements are affected by our relationship to and interactions with each other.

> Very little that is positive is solitary. When was the last time you laughed uproariously? The last time you felt indescribable joy? The last time you sensed profound meaning and purpose? The last time you felt enormously proud of an accomplishment? Even without knowing the particulars of these high points of your life, I know their form: all of them took place around other people. Other people are the best antidote to the downs of life and the single most reliable up.[4]

Seligman's work on what drives well-being is instructive about how to flourish. His emphasis on the importance of positive relationships and meaning-making are supported by new research on mitigating secondary trauma and promoting resilience that suggests community is essential. This is further underscored by what we've learned from students, human rights practitioners, and content moderators: that taking in trauma alone is much more difficult than doing so with even one other person. Figure 5.1.

But what makes community protective? Is a predominantly digital community as protective as one in the physical world?

---

[2] Rachel Naomi Remen, *Kitchen Table Wisdom: Stories that Heal* (New York: Macmillan 1996).
[3] Martin E. P. Seligman, *Flourish* (New York: Atria Paperback 2013).
[4] Ibid. at 20.

FIGURE 5.1 Students in the Human Rights Center Investigations Lab pose in front of the lab's unofficial motto, which underscores the importance of community to wellbeing. Source: Photo by Andrea Lampros

Meta CEO Mark Zuckerberg asserts that Meta's Facebook platform was built to strengthen community and offer a collective experience of our world. After coming under fire for the platform's complicity in misinformation campaigns related to the 2016 Trump-Biden presidential election, Zuckerberg heralded Facebook's digital communities for their potential to do everything from combat climate change and end poverty, to spread tolerance. In 2017, Zuckerberg declared of Facebook: "We have a responsibility to do more, not just to connect the world but to bring the world closer together. … We want to help one billion people join meaningful communities,"[5] articulating the company's public-facing mission at a post-election high point of national polarization and rancor. "Right now, I think the most important thing we can do is bring people closer together."

Regardless of the platform's stated intentions, however, research indicates that people are actually more socially and politically divided today than they were before the rise of social media – with young people especially feeling isolated, even before the onset of the pandemic.[6] Psychologists Jonathan Haidt and Jean M. Twenge have illuminated the ways teenagers in particular have become more socially isolated since the onset of the smartphone and especially since platforms like Facebook and Instagram began to use the "like" button.[7] In a paper they published in the *Journal of Adolescence*, Haidt and Twenge report that in thirty-six out of thirty-seven countries loneliness at school [has] steadily increased between 2012, when smartphones first became accessible globally, and 2018.[8]

[5] Josh Constine, "Facebook Changes Mission Statement to 'Bring the World Closer Together'," *Tech Crunch*, June 22, 2017.
[6] Jonathan Haidt and Jean M. Twenge, "This Is Our Chance to Pull Teenagers out of the Smartphone Trap," *New York Times*, July 31, 2021.
[7] Ibid.
[8] Jean M. Twenge, Jonathan Haidt, Andrea B. Blake, Cooper McAllister, Hannah Lemon, and Astrid Le Roy, "Worldwide Increases in Adolescent Loneliness," 93 *Journal of Adolescence* 264 (2021).

Their findings were based on a survey administered by the Programme for International Student Assessment to more than one million fifteen- and sixteen-year-old students around the world, which was designed to measure loneliness at school. The survey was administered in 2000, 2003, 2012, 2015, and 2018. When comparing loneliness measures between 2012 and 2018, the researchers found that almost twice as many of the students "had elevated levels of school loneliness," with the effects largest among girls, and the rates of loneliness being highest when smartphone and Internet use were high. Their findings paralleled a documented trend in the United States of "loneliness, depression and self-harm increas[ing] sharply among U.S. adolescents" beginning in the early 2010s.[9]

Importantly, the researchers found that such trends affect not just the students who frequently use social media and the Internet more generally but also their peers. As they've written, "Social interaction involves a group, not just an individual, and the average adolescent in 2018 had fewer opportunities to socialize in person and more opportunities to socialize online than the average adolescent in 2000 due to the shift in social norms. Thus, at the group level, they had less opportunity for … in-person social interaction … that protects against loneliness, and more opportunity for an activity that does not," such as digital media use. As they explain, such "social norm shifts may impact teens no matter how much or how little they personally use digital media. For example, social media may heighten feelings of missing out both when adolescents do not use it [as then they are cut off from communication] and when they do use it," as they may observe what their friends are doing without them and feel excluded.[10]

In 2021, the *Wall Street Journal* published a damning set of articles based on a series of Facebook leaks. As later reported in *The Guardian*, Facebook's own researchers had discovered that Instagram (a Facebook product) "make[s] body images worse for one in three girls" and that 13 percent of British and 6 percent of American teens who reported suicidal thoughts traced those thoughts to their time on Instagram, in part due to their feelings of inferiority when comparing their looks to others on the platform.[11]

Of course, the negative aspects of social media don't just extend to teenagers. A consortium of researchers led by Amy Ostertun Geirdal conducted a cross-country comparative study of people in Norway, the United States, the United Kingdom, and Australia, to see how those peoples' use of social media was affecting their mental health during the pandemic – a time of especially acute and widespread social isolation.[12] They surveyed 3,810 people across the four countries, 80 percent of whom were female but otherwise representative based on age and education level,

[9] Ibid.
[10] Ibid.
[11] Dan Milmo and Clea Skopeliti, "Teenage Girls, Body Image and Instagram's 'Perfect Storm'," *The Guardian*, September 18, 2021.
[12] Amy Ostertun Geirdal, Mary Ruffolo, Janni Leung, Hilde Thygesen, Daicia Price, Tore Bonsaksen, and Mariyana Schoultz, "Mental Health, Quality of Life, Wellbeing, Loneliness and Use of Social Media in a Time of Social Distancing during the COVID-19 Outbreak. A Cross-country Comparative Study," 30 *Journal of Mental Health* 1 (2021).

and found that 50–74 percent showed a "high" level of emotional distress, with Norwegians suffering the least at 50 percent, those from the United Kingdom suffering the most at 74 percent, and the United States a close second, with 70 percent of respondents reporting emotional distress during the two-month period under consideration. Importantly, the researchers found that high-frequent use of social media during the pandemic was associated with poorer mental and psychosocial health. According to the researchers, 75.8 percent of those surveyed who reported using social media several times per day were classified with emotional distress and 75.6 percent with poor overall quality of life.[13] While for most, this distress was situational and thus long-term outcomes could be expected to be more positive, the interaction of social media use with social distancing is of particular relevance to this book.

It's always difficult to know what causes what: Does higher use of social media lead to poorer mental outcomes? Or does poorer mental well-being drive higher levels of social media use? In trying to explain differences between nationalities, the researchers theorized that some of the distress might have been related to the level of trust or mistrust participants had in their governments, including their assessment of how their country was handling the lockdowns.

Citing a 2014 study about trust, researcher Geirdal explains that "mistrust can depend on formal and informal information and communication, doubt about (changing) health care recommendations and media's role in publishing misinterpretation and misbelief in science. The differences may also be due to cultural considerations, familial, relational or socio-political differences,"[14] including countries' willingness to provide benefits to those who fall ill and the degree of paid leave afforded by workplaces. Importantly, the researchers pointed out, such sociopolitical differences may "mirror a feeling of safety or insecurity, trust or lack of trust in the particular situation, and may be an explanation of the reported differences in psychosocial factors."[15] Interestingly, the researchers also found that people tended to be less worried about their own health and more worried about their family members, showing the extent to which stress, well-being, and other factors relate to our connections to others – and not just ourselves.

Ultimately, those in the Geirdal study who used social media frequently were found to have poorer mental health, quality of life, and well-being, as well as greater loneliness, than those who used social media less frequently. However, the researchers also theorized that peoples' wellness may have an iterative effect in their engagement with social media, noting that while "frequent use of social media seems to have a negative impact of mental and psychosocial health, conversely, people with better mental health may seek and find more joy, distraction, recreation and relaxation in their more limited use of social media."[16]

---

[13] Ibid. at 5.
[14] Geirdal et al, "Mental Health" (citing J. Q. Liao and R. Fielding, "Uncertain News: Trust and Preventive Practices in Respiratory Infectious Diseases," 19 *European Psychologist* 4–12 (2014).
[15] Ibid.
[16] Ibid.

While many studies underscore the negative effects of social media on happiness, research also indicates that true social connection to others (especially in our offline lives) can mitigate those effects. Indeed, many users are drawn to social media and other online communities and interactions *for* the sense of community that has been implicitly or explicitly promised. How can we magnify that sense of connection, both with the content and our interpersonal engagement? For example, do algorithms that prioritize the posts of more frequent users potentially miss the boat on increasing connections with people with fewer followers? Or are those lighter social media users actually the most satisfied, because of the strength of their ties to those with whom they're connected online? Maybe the person who rarely tweets/posts is the person who most needs their posts seen? Or maybe the person who has only 50 friends on Facebook is actually far less lonely than the person with 500?

Relationships also protect from psychosocial harm in other contexts. For example, a study of adults aged 50–105 years (with an average age of 69) has demonstrated the importance of social connection to minimize the negative effects of exposure to trauma.[17] The study looked at how social connection affected the mental health of individuals who were exposed to war-related events related to the Israel–Palestine conflict, such as missile attacks, relatively late in life. The researchers found a strong protective effect in human connection: "Practitioners should be aware of the protective role of social connectedness in the context of warfare exposure in old age and intervention programs with this population should strive towards bolstering social connections."[18] If social media can isolate us but in person social connection tends to ward off the negative effects of exposure to trauma, does it follow that taking in violent or emotionally charged information is less harmful when done collectively or in community?

We have anecdotal evidence that the answer is "yes." The experiences of the "content moderators" working for big tech companies such as YouTube, Facebook, and Twitter provide an extreme, but instructive, example for all of us who view graphic or traumatic content on the Internet. These content moderators – often outsourced workers or temps – are charged with looking at and assessing every piece of violent or pornographic or hateful content that appears in their often overflowing queues to determine whether it should stay online or be taken down. The reflections of content moderators we interviewed and those who have spoken publicly about their work underscore the importance of community when viewing graphic content and the perils of doing so alone.

Oakland native AnaStacia Nicol Wright worked as a content moderator for a year and a half through a temp agency before attending law school. She is now a staff attorney for a Bay Area firm called Worksafe that defends the rights of workers. As part of her training as a content moderator on her first day at work – without any preparation or details about what type of "sensitive content" she would be viewing –

---

[17] E. Schwartz and A. Shrira, "Social Connectedness Moderates the Relationship Between Warfare Exposure, PTSD Symptoms, and Health among Older Adults," 82 *Psychiatry* 158–172 (2019).
[18] Ibid.

Wright joined colleagues gathered around a computer. Pictures of naked prepubes-cent girls popped onto the screen. She quickly figured out that she would be working on the CSAI – Child Sexual Abuse Investigations – team.

Without warning on day-one of her job, Wright says, she was in the company's workflow, watching a kind of violence and depravity she never knew existed. "I remember just leaving the room that day and crying," recalls Wright. "I was like 'What the fuck?' People are just so sick. That was my first day." She said she didn't cry in front of her new co-workers but broke down when she was finally alone at her desk.

With time, however, the community of co-workers she found at the company kept her going. Wright said her teammates provided much-needed practical support that was good for both efficiency and protection. For example, a single video depicting child abuse might circulate over and over again. If some of Wright's teammates had already seen the video, they could vouch for it and relieve her of the burden of view-ing. Wright said her CSAI team worked in a common room and gave each other much-needed social and emotional support as well.

Liz Scott,[19] who worked first as a content moderator and eventually managed a content moderation team at YouTube, said the company was a bit ahead of the curve in some of its protocols for easing the effects of traumatic material – including the practice of enabling people to work collectively. The value comes from people supporting each other and "being able to say quickly, 'Hey, what do you think about this?'" she said. "I think there were some really good managers early on in 2010, who were just like 'We need to fight for this [type of community and collective support].' I think it just got progressively harder to protect that at scale [the opportunity to work in teams] and fight for that at scale."

Michael Shaw, the clinical psychologist who works with photojournalists and other visual professionals, shared an example of the power of community. At the height of COVID, a photographer covering the lockdown in New York City reached out to him. As someone with plenty of experience documenting social crises, she could not understand why she was having so much trouble keeping her focus. More unusually, she found herself over-identifying with her subjects.

> Because prevention knowledge was as hard to come by as proper protection gear, I thought she was afraid for her safety. Or perhaps, she was anxious because she had family members in the same circumstances. A recurring theme in our calls, though, was her frustration that she couldn't hang out with her photographer friends. And even though she was seeing them on Zoom, it 'wasn't like really see-ing them.' Because she had never lacked for that kind of contact before, she never appreciated how much she used peer support to maintain her objectivity. What she also found surprising is that several of her colleague-friends were experiencing the same thing. So from then on, she doubled down on her in-person peer support—mostly outdoors and six feet apart, of course.

---

[19] A pseudonym.

Emiliana Simon-Thomas is the science director of the Greater Good Science Center, a research institute based at UC Berkeley that studies "the science of a meaningful life," including explorations of the span of emotions at play in our world. She believes that when it comes to health and well-being, focusing on relationships can be more important than strategies that focus on one's self, such as meditation or therapy. She highlighted a study of combat soldiers who developed strong family-like bonds in the course of their collective deployment during conflicts. Their social bonds, strengthened by their shared experiences, lessened the trauma of violence.

Further underscoring the power of social connection, studies indicate that military drone operators experience post-traumatic stress at rates as high or higher than combat soldiers.[20] A comparative study of 670 drone pilots and 751 manned-aircraft pilots found that 5 percent of drone pilots displayed symptoms that placed them at high risk of PTSD,[21] versus 1 percent of manned-aircraft pilots.[22] According to the study's authors, drone personnel reported suffering high emotional distress, including "anxiety, depression, emotional adjustment difficulties" severe enough to suggest a need for mental health care.[23] Similarly, a study by Joseph Ouma, Wayne Chappelle, and Amber Salinas found that "approximately one out of every five active duty drone operators were twice as likely to report high levels of emotional exhaustion when compared with National Guard/Reserve operators."[24]

One factor in the high rates of PTSD/PTSI among drone operators may be the lack of family-like connections and social support afforded to combat soldiers, who develop deep relationships while deployed with their teams.[25] Drone operators, by contrast, often go to war essentially alone. Instead of deploying with their unit to a foreign country, they frequently work from an office near their hometown, where they study their targets, eventually receive orders to shoot, and then review the aftermath in tremendous detail on a screen so they can report the results to their superiors. They can be home in time for dinner, in the company of friends and family who have no idea what they've just witnessed and who have never experienced a similar traumatic event.

Surveillance and Reconnaissance Wing surgeon Cameron Thurmon, who oversaw a team of doctors and psychologists in charge of mental health for the drone

---

[20] Peter M. Asaro, "The Labor of Surveillance and Bureaucratized Killing: New Subjectivities of Military Drone Operators," 23 *Social Semiotics* 217 (2013).

[21] Alex Edney-Browne, "Embodiment and Affect in a Digital Age: Understanding Mental Illness among Military Drone Personnel," *Krisis Journal for Contemporary Philosophy* (2017), available at: https://archive.krisis.eu/embodiment-and-affect-in-a-digital-age/ (citing Wayne Chappelle and Kent McDonald, "Prevalence of High Emotional Distress and Symptoms of Post-traumatic Stress Disorder in US Air Force Active Duty Remotely Piloted Aircraft Operators," Air Force Research Laboratory Report (2012): 6).

[22] Ibid.

[23] Ibid.

[24] Ibid. (citing Joseph A. Ouma, Wayne Chappelle and Amber Salinas, "Facets of Occupational Burnout among U.S. Air Force Active Duty and National Guard/Reserve MQ-1 Predator and MQ-9 Reaper Operators," Air Force Research Laboratory Report (2011): 12).

[25] See, for example, Rajiv Kumar Saini, M. S. V. K. Raju, and Amit Chail, "Cry in the Sky: Psychological Impact on Drone Operators," 30 *Industrial Psychiatry Journal* S15–S19 (2021).

unit, told NPR: "You don't need a fancy study to tell you that watching someone beheaded, or skinned alive, or tortured to death [even if remote], is gonna have an impact on you as a human being. Everybody understands that. What was not widely understood is the level of exposure that our wing has to that type of incident. We see it all. ... There are some things you just can't unsee."[26] And without the community afforded by a squadron embedded in a combat setting that is physical and not virtual, there is a greater risk of secondary trauma or PTSD/PTSI.

UC Irvine Criminology Professor Keramet Reiter has seen the need for and power of community and connection among some of the most vulnerable and traumatized people in the world: inmates in solitary confinement in California's supermax prisons. Those prisoners who survive with the "least trauma and damage," she told us, "are those who write letters to people on the outside and, through a network of correspondence, maintain an active social web or set of bonds."

Interestingly, even though Reiter recognized the need for social support and connection among people who are incarcerated, she didn't initially recognize this same need within herself or her students. She would sometimes spend eight hours a day with people in solitary confinement, breathing in their stories and the extreme conditions they endured. Her only exhale would be a glass of wine and a talk with her psychiatrist husband at the end of the day. In 2017, she trained eight doctoral students to conduct interviews with more than 200 people who were incarcerated. Many of her students had been personally touched by the US prison system in some way, with family members or friends who had been imprisoned. Their personal identities were enmeshed with the work – a factor that can raise vulnerability to distress. Reiter said she was consumed with preparing the students to conduct the interviews. While she focused on interview methods and logistics, her students' emotional needs weren't initially on her radar.

After the interviews were completed, the students expressed being emotionally overwhelmed by their conversations with people who were incarcerated – their stories of pain and hopelessness were difficult to bear. In response to their distress, Reiter organized a session to debrief. When the students came for lunch at her house, she realized that they were all showing signs of secondary trauma. For example, some said they didn't want to touch their family members; others felt agitated and isolated. "It was a real wake-up moment for me," said Reiter, who has since infused every project with attention to fostering social connection and resiliency among her students. She now insists that some portion of the funds that are awarded for her research be used for social gatherings for the students as a means of cultivating community and support.

Of course, community can extend beyond just your immediate circle. As Emily and Amelia Nagoski have explained in their book *Burnout*, which acknowledges the importance of relationships to our well-being, "Humans are not built to function

---

[26] McCammon, "The Warfare May Be Remote but the Trauma Is Real," *National Public Radio*, April 24, 2017.

autonomously; we are built to oscillate from connection to autonomy and back again. Connection – with friends, family, pets, the divine, etc. – is as necessary as food and water."[27]

Alexa realized the importance of relationships to her own resiliency when participating in an assignment we had created with one of our student team leads for our lab students. The assignment asked people to take part in a quick exercise that requires reflecting for a couple of minutes on "what they bring" to doing human rights work and "what they receive" in return. What individuals "bring" to such work may include skills as diverse as speaking the language of those most impacted, to having advanced abilities to find information online, to knowing how to scrape social media, while what they "receive" ranges from a byline (if a journalist), or academic units (if a student), or payment (if staff). To the prompts, Alexa was surprised to find herself responding "everything" as an answer to what she gave, and "community" to what she received in return.

To this day, when she finds herself struggling to maintain her own resiliency, she looks to both of these prompts. If her answer to what she gives is "everything," she knows it's important to focus on other aspects of her life and identity – spending more time with her kids, for example, or hiking with friends. And if her answer to what she gets starts to feel like "nothing," she knows it's time to reach out to others and strengthen her sense of connection with colleagues, which is what she especially values from the work.

For Sam Dubberley, who has pioneered resiliency methods through his work as a journalist and with Amnesty International, it's important to see community in all of its forms. "I always thought community meant absolutely everybody, and now for me it doesn't mean that." He explained that collectively experiencing traumatic digital content with one or two other people can make it easier to take. From his time at Eurovision through his work with students at Amnesty International and now with his team at Human Rights Watch, he has encouraged colleagues and students to look at difficult photos and videos with at least one other person and to build some form of community within the team.

So what can we do as everyday users to leverage the power of community to mitigate the potential negative effects of engaging with upsetting graphic content on social media? The people we spoke with as well as existing research strongly suggest that the following can help.

Talk with others about what you've seen: And then talk with them about the larger social issues that the graphic content reflects. Maybe we can't "unsee" disturbing videos or photos or push away knowledge of hateful misinformation that has overwhelmed our social media platforms, but we can all discuss it. Researchers say releasing negative feelings and not bottling them up after viewing something intense can help to dissipate potential long-term effects. The person you talk with

[27] Nagoski and Nagoski, *Burnout*, 215.

may be someone close to you, a colleague, a psychologist, or others. Talking with trained therapists can be incredibly helpful for some people but of course is not always an option. Meg Satterthwaite says that in the absence of access to expert mental health support, "peer-to-peer" efforts that train people how to actively listen to each other (taking in information with full attention) can really make a difference. Often, she says, people don't need a response or a solution. They just need to air a feeling or experience. If you are routinely viewing graphic images in a professional setting, it may help to launch a peer counseling program. If your engagement is personal, you may want to seek out friends or colleagues who are good listeners or provide others with that support. Of course, if you are sharing a photo or video with a friend or colleague, it's critical to communicate what they are about to see with specific information so that you minimize the risk of harm to them and so that they can make an informed decision about whether to look or watch. Saying that something is graphic isn't enough. If there's violence against children or blood or intense emotion, it's important to mention such details. Enabling someone to prepare for what they're about to see can mute the element of surprise and allow them to take steps to mitigate the intensity of their exposure.

Watch or look with others: Despite the stated objectives of social media platforms to bring people together in community, as we've seen, research tells us that viewing social media is often a solitary experience and can be isolating. Having hundreds of friends or followers on social media might be validating, but such surface connections shouldn't be mistaken for community. Human rights researchers and journalists are increasingly working in pairs and teams as they grapple with the worst kinds of social media imagery. Professionally, this strengthens our work because multiple perspectives and eyes inevitably bring more insights. On a personal level, taking in disturbing images with a loved one, friend, or colleague enables a collective experience and the potential for expressing collective grief. Grief expert David Kessler talked about "collective grief" in the context of the pandemic: "This is hitting us and we're grieving. Collectively. We are not used to this kind of collective grief in the air."[28]

We all frequently sit alone with our phones, sometimes engaging in what's called "doom scrolling," through one negative post after another.[29] It's not likely that we'll go back to the days of sitting with our family watching the nightly news. But something in that bygone equation of collective viewing – resulting in collective awe, like when Olympic gymnast Nadia Comaneci stuck her landing for a perfect 10, or times of collective horror, as when the *Challenger* space shuttle exploded – provided us with some protection. Today, algorithms are placing us in different information bubbles; the four family members crowded around a dinner table may have seen very different information about the world that day, given their different

---

[28] Scott Berinato, "That Discomfort You're Feeling Is Grief," *Harvard Business Review*, March 23, 2020.
[29] Shelby Deering, "Mental Health A-Z: What Is Doomscrolling?," verywellmind, January 3, 2021.

demographics. How can we begin to replicate some of our past togetherness with our twenty-first century ways of learning about the world?

Find ways to have community, in real life: The virtual worlds we dwell in so often, exacerbated during the pandemic years, can simultaneously bring us intimately close to seeing pain and suffering and yet remove us from actual people. Even though video conferencing or chatting is technically still virtual, it's a step more intimate and interactive than posting and waiting for likes on social media. In pandemic surges, platforms like Zoom (like it or hate it) have brought old friends and extended family together in sometimes unprecedented ways. One of the first group investigations our student team tackled during the COVID-19 pandemic was monitoring cities across the United States for violence should it erupt on the November 2020 election night. Our team worked on their individual investigative tasks in parallel, with a Zoom room open. When someone had a strong reaction to a piece of online content, that content and reaction could be shared with others. People could "step out" into breakout rooms to discuss the information or their feelings or pivot to another task. While it wasn't a perfect substitute for working together in the same room, eating pizza and sipping sodas, we could still have a real-time conversation with others who understood what we were going through. Sometimes we were quiet, and sometimes we talked over each other, but there was a sense of collective experience that protected us from what we witnessed. It also allowed us to have clear "start and end times" and provided some outside accountability to make sure we were taking breaks. While those breaks weren't always taken, Zoom allowed us to watch out for each other, both literally and figuratively. Ultimately, video chatting can enable people with similar passions and interests to connect, regardless of geography, often even expanding their communities.

6

Meaning in Our Online Lives

Eric Stover, a veteran war crimes investigator and faculty director of the UC Berkeley Human Rights Center, spent much of his professional life leading forensic teams in the investigation of those missing due to political repression or war. One of the most important lessons he learned was the need to work closely with local human rights organizations and to place the families of the disappeared and their needs at the center of every investigation. Unlike students who interface with graphic digital content, Stover has almost always worked in person with the survivors and their families.

During the 1990s, for example, Stover and forensic anthropologist Clyde Snow trained a team of Guatemalan archeology and anthropology students in the exhumation of mass graves believed to contain the remains of opponents to the military regime. During the exhumations, Stover observed how family members from nearby villages, especially women, would cluster near a mass grave as the students began an excavation. At first, the women – many of whom had slipped into what Stover describes as a limbo world of hope and denial – were reluctant to speak to the student scientists. But, after a day or so, a group of women would draw near. A widow might produce a photograph of her husband and recount how he had been taken away by soldiers late one night and never seen again. Often, in the mornings, the women would kneel next to the grave and say a prayer for the deceased and later cook a meal for the students. As the day wore on, men would come in from the fields and volunteer to heft buckets of earth out of the grave and help the students cover the open pits with tarps and carry their shovels and picks back to the village. Once the dead had been identified, the students would return to the village to attend the funerals of the deceased.[1]

For years – even decades – the Guatemalan government had denied families any information about the whereabouts of their loved ones. In the presence of the

---

[1] See Eric Stover and Rachell Shigekane, "Exhumation of Mass Graves: Balancing Legal and Humanitarian Needs," in Eric Stover and Harvey W. Weinstein (eds), *My Neighbor, My Enemy: Justice and Community in the Aftermath of Mass Atrocity* (Cambridge: Cambridge University Press 2004): 85–103.

student investigators whose sole aim was to establish the truth, the relatives could begin to regain a sense of control by helping in the process of locating their missing relatives. At the same time, the young scientists were giving families the opportunity to provide their loved ones with proper burial and, in some cases, justice. For Stover and the students, the interactions with family members of the missing brought them great meaning and served to underscore the importance of their grueling work.

In today's digital world, Stover wonders if investigating atrocities online – whether they are videos of the horrors of the Syrian conflict or racist attacks in the United States – can yield the same kind of meaning for social media investigators that he and his teammates experienced and continue to experience conducting investigations on the ground in places like Guatemala or in the United States (as with Stover's recent work to investigate the Tulsa Race Massacre of 1921). Observing graphic digital content doesn't provide investigators with the same reciprocity.

When we observe a graphic video, such as an attack on a hospital in Ukraine, for example, we are likely to be alone in witnessing pain without having direct contact with the survivors and the family members of those who died. Researchers and activists are now exploring how we – as journalists, advocates, or simply as social media users – can better acquire meaning similar to what Stover and his teammates experienced during forensic investigations in Guatemala and other war-affected countries.

Finding meaning requires a deeper consideration for each of us. What matters to us? How can grappling with humanity's pain actually strengthen us as humans? Finding a sense of satisfaction – even in the ongoing struggle against oppression – is no small task and yet is essential to the change we may seek to make in the world. Understanding *why* we are looking and why we are looking away when we do can give us clarity and enable us to be more intentional about our news intake.

There's an important difference between looking at images of atrocity for increased social awareness and looking at such images as a form of what's colloquially known as "war porn." The term was notably discussed by French theorist Jean Baudrillard in an essay with the same name,[2] in which he explained how war images from Iraq "borrowed from the aesthetics and production values of modern pornography."[3] Much like the tendency to rubberneck during a car accident, the term has since been used to describe "the huge amounts of garish video material and photographs that emanate from wars fought in the digital age."[4] Or, per another commentator, "war porn" can be used to reference "any image or video produced

---

[2] J. Baudrillard, "War Porn," in Sylvère Lotringer (ed.), *The Conspiracy of Art: Manifestos, Interviews, Essays* (New York: Semiotext(e) 2005): 205–209.

[3] PBS, "When Does War Become Pornography?," *Frontline*, available at: www.pbs.org/wgbh/pages/frontline/digitalnation/waging-war/a-new-generation/war-porn.html?play.

[4] Ibid.

FIGURE 6.1 Trump supporters swarm the US Capitol in Washington DC on January 6, 2021. Five people died during the riot.
Source: Photo by Lev Radin; Shutterstock

in a combat zone depicting death, violence, gore, brutality, depravity, lewd behavior or any other shocking act that would be perceived unacceptable or even criminal if committed on American soil."[5] Even Sontag has referred to war as having, at least for some, a "perennial seductiveness,"[6] noting that "all images that display the violation of an attractive body are, to a certain degree, pornographic. But images of the repulsive can also allure."[7]

Such material can be titillating or fascinating, and for some, looking at it can become obsessive; entire websites have been established to help "traffic" such imagery, including sites like gotwarporn.com and the now-defunct nowthatsfuckedup.com, which was taken down under accusations of "misdemeanor obscenity"[8] – essentially accusations that the material is illegal because it is obscene. Some commentators have argued that despite the shock value, such images may give soldiers and others who feel a kinship with the perpetrators a temporary high by providing a gratifying sense of strength, dominance, and moral superiority (for example, to American soldiers and others who identify with the US military when Americans are the perpetrators, as with the Abu Ghraib photos, or those who identify with President Trump, when viewing photos of the rioting at the US Capitol on January 6, 2021 – Figure 6.1). This may be especially true during a time of cultural transition during which wealthy, white, and/or non-immigrant Americans who have long been socially powerful may feel especially vulnerable.[9]

[5] Matthis Chiroux, "Is Our Military Addicted to 'War Porn'?," *HuffPost*, January 15, 2012.
[6] Sontag, *Regarding the Pain of Others*, 122.
[7] Ibid. at 95.
[8] Chris Wilson, "What Happened to NTFU? Here's Your Answer," Documenting Reality, www.documentingreality.com/forum/view.php?pg=ntfu
[9] Matthew Chiroux, "Is Our Military Addicted to War Porn?" *Huffington Post*, January 15, 2012.

Of course, this raises the question: What does it mean to have a meaningful social interaction? And is that possible online? In 2020, researchers set out to answer these questions. They administered a survey to approximately 5,000 people, roughly split across three countries: the United States, Japan, and India.[10] They found that three variables typically determined when respondents found an engagement was meaning-ful: (1) the people involved, (2) the activities they participated in, and (3) the impact of the interaction – specifically, what resulted from the interaction. Ultimately, the researchers concluded that it was the third variable – the impact of the interaction – that was most likely to determine whether an interaction would be deemed mean-ingful ("for example, it brought them 'closer' with [a] person or because that person 'taught' them or because they were able to 'help' that person out").[11] Impact was typi-cally described as one of three kinds – emotional, informational, or tangible – with the first two being most prevalent. When it came to emotional impact, "people high-lighted feelings experienced or witnessed, typically in the form of empathy, love, trust or care that led to a change in mood or the strengthening of a relationship," while informational impact "happened when knowledge, advice, or a better understanding was developed."[12] When respondents described an interaction as not meaningful, they often discussed the interaction as having a lack of impact, using phrases like "trivial, small talk, nothing to offer, not genuine, only for timepass, and a waste of time."[13] Ultimately, the "single factor that most distinguished meaningful interac-tions from non-meaningful ones was that meaningful interactions had an impact that respondents felt went beyond the interaction itself to enhance their lives, the lives of their interaction partners, or their relationships."[14]

The researchers also looked at whether the medium of communication had an impact on whether an interaction was deemed meaningful. They found that ulti-mately meaning depended more on factors such as who was involved than the medium of communication – although synchronous interactions were often judged as more meaningful than asynchronous ones.[15] The researchers ultimately concluded that while earlier research found in-person interactions to be more meaningful than online interactions, today it may make more sense to "think about communication media through affordances and capabilities (eg, synchronicity, ability to engage in activities) rather than as a factor on its own."[16] Indeed, they found that nearly one quarter of those they surveyed reported their most recent meaningful social

---

[10] Eden Litt, Siyan Zhao, Robert Kraut, and Moira Burke, "What Are Meaningful Social Interactions in Today's Media Landscape? A Cross-Cultural Survey," 6 *Social Media and Society* 4 (2020).

[11] Ibid. at 8.

[12] Ibid. at 9.

[13] Ibid. at 8.

[14] Ibid. at 9.

[15] Ibid. Of course, digital communications reside along a spectrum of synchronicity, with text messag-ing in real time closer to a phone call, while text messaging with hours or days-long delays between messages closer to an asynchronous post.

[16] Litt et al, "What Are Meaningful Social Interactions?," 12.

interaction having happened on a social media platform – and that such interactions were rated as meaningful as those that occurred face-to-face.[17]

The writer and activist Adrienne Maree Brown has tapped into the deep societal pain of racial violence, environmental peril, and civic disunity, to probe this question of how we find meaning and sometimes even joy in engaging with the painful struggle for justice. Like the founders of RatedR, she proposes that we get beyond sacrificing ourselves to make change; past the cancel culture that thrives in digital spaces and that pushes us away from and not toward each other; and even beyond the concept of mitigating trauma when witnessing violence. Brown is good with traditional notions of resilience ("a bath, centering, cooking ... singing really loudly")[18] but also asks, "How do we have a *transformative* resilience?." She explains that the concept of transformative resilience is about more than simply minimizing harm, recovering from violence, or going back to exploitative conditions.

> It's hard in a city like Detroit because resilience can be weaponized. Like if people like you bounce back from anything, we'll just keep doing anything to you. We'll add an incinerator to your neighborhood or whatever; you'll be fine. And so I think there's something about, 'How do we have a *transformative* resilience?' How do we have resilience that is not just like we can recover back to conditions that we weren't very happy with in the first place. ... that's beyond my own origin, you know like I need to recover something that goes back past the many hours that my grandmother overworked, and I need to recover something that goes back past my enslaved ancestors, and recover something that goes back past my kidnapped ancestors ... like I feel this long, long, long arc of the work that I'm in right now. Almost everyone that came before me was trying to work towards some joy, some freedom, some sense of safety for their children and themselves. And now I am awakened. I am aware of all of that and I have an option in front of me to be resilient across time and space. And that feels very exciting.[19]

This concept of "transformative resilience" relates to our ability to connect with the complex and painful events playing out every minute in our world – events that may be a daily reality for some (like racialized police violence) or that penetrate second hand. Connecting with painful stories without growing numb and viewing the news with the intention of moving more deeply into our shared humanity are monumental and elusive challenges. To start, there is much we can learn from the science of

---

[17] Ibid. The researchers give an example of a meaningful social interaction that took place on social media, quoting the following response: "My most meaningful recent social interaction was with a friend I had known for years but we lost touch. We recently reconnected on Facebook and we both reminisced about the past and caught up about what we were up to. It was meaningful because I felt very connected to my past and present self."

[18] adrienne maree brown, "a range of reflections on resilience," available at: http://adriennemareebrown .net/2016/11/09/a-range-of-reflections-on-resilience/ (last visited July 12, 2022).

[19] "Pleasure Activism: Change That Nourishes You – with adrienne maree brown," available at: www .youtube.com/watch?v=QSP6s2ZEJJs&ab_channel=NeilSattin.

empathy and happiness, fields of study that focus on what these positive emotions are and how they can be facilitated.

UC Berkeley's Greater Good Science Center has been at the forefront of this work since 2001. The center delves into what it calls the "science of a meaningful life," conducting scientific research into emotions like awe, empathy, and happiness, and making their findings accessible to non-academics through articles, podcasts, and workshops. The center goes beyond "self-help" to look at the social psychology of well-being to generate insights and tactics that anyone can use.

"The Greater Good's perspective really focuses on the importance of social experiences, of the quality of relationships, of one's tendency toward generosity and cooperation, and of one's sense of meaningful belonging as sources of well being, particularly the sources that can change well being in real time," explained Emiliana Simon-Thomas, the Greater Good's science director.

Simon-Thomas said her center examines how we can avoid a downward spiral or grow numb from distressing experiences including secondary trauma, and instead find meaning and develop a deeper kind of contentment. This project is based on the ideas of positive psychology – the scientific study of well-being, and ultimately, what makes life worth living.[20] "How do you think in more optimistic ways? How do you connect with your sense of purpose and belonging? How do you cultivate resilience, grounded in skills of self-awareness and self-compassion?" Simon-Thomas explains that cognitive behavioral therapy can help us adjust our thought patterns to bolster self-worth and give us hope that "things can be better in the future than they are in the moment."

MEANING THROUGH GRIEF AND JOY

Focusing on grief, and the process of moving through the various stages of grief, can also help inform how to land somewhere more positive. Psychiatrist Elisabeth Kübler-Ross famously developed her theory of the stages of grief in the late 1960s in response to her observations of the emotional states of dying patients. She theorized that those experiencing grief will typically cycle through denial, anger, bargaining, depression, and acceptance.[21] In the midst of the pandemic, grief expert David Kessler approached Kübler-Ross's family about adding a potential sixth step: meaning. In discussing the addition, Kessler specifically cited the relationship of people to technology and to other humans: "I had talked to Elisabeth quite a bit about what came after acceptance. I did not want to stop at acceptance when I experienced

---

[20] Positive psychology's Seligman similarly emphasizes that meaning, which he defines as "belonging to and serving something that you believe is bigger than the self," is a cornerstone of well-being. He says the goal of positive psychology is to increase the amount of "flourishing" in life, which (like the Nagoskis) he distinguishes from happiness. Seligman, *Flourish*, 17.

[21] Elisabeth Kubler-Ross, *On Death and Dying: What the Dying Have to Teach Doctors, Nurses, Clergy and Their Own Families* (Scribner 2014).

some personal grief. I wanted meaning in those darkest hours. And I do believe we find light in those times. Even now people are realizing they can connect through technology. They are not as remote as they thought. They are realizing they can use their phones for long conversations. They're appreciating walks. I believe we will continue to find meaning now and when this is over."

Psychologists have long acknowledged the importance of rituals, for example, funerals, to mark the end of a life and to facilitate the process of grieving. In this same way, it can be equally important to mark the end of an online investigation or the viewing of an upsetting video. Such markers can be as simple as stepping outside for a moment, reflecting on what you've learned, considering what you might do with that information (if anything), and remembering to breathe. For teams, it may mean taking a moment to debrief on the experience or to celebrate a milestone in the form of a dinner or other gathering.

Grief and joy may seem like polar opposite emotions, but in their depth, the experience can be comparable. Both emotions can be consuming and life-changing. And grief and joy are deeply relevant to our experience of relating to the world.

Emily and Amelia Nagoski have written extensively on how to foster joy. As they explain, joy is ultimately a very different emotion than happiness, the latter being what people often claim to be seeking in online spaces. "Happiness is predicated on 'happenings,' on what's occurring, on whether your life is going right and whether all is well. Joy arises from an internal clarity about … purpose. When we engage with something larger than ourselves, we make meaning; and when we can resonate, bell-like, with that Something Larger, that's joy," they write.[22] Importantly, that sense of joy, unlike happiness, is independent of what we are exposed to, and is instead related to why we are exposing ourselves to difficult information in the first place, and what we choose to do with what we encounter. As they elaborate, this is good news: "Because that Something Larger is within us, no external circumstances can take away our source of joy, no matter the 'happenings' around us."[23]

Frank Ochberg, the psychiatrist who specializes in post-traumatic stress, has given a lot of thought to how to strengthen peoples' sense of joy and well-being, especially that of reporters and others who regularly confront tragedy and may be especially at risk of secondary trauma or post-traumatic stress injury. In order to help people feel emotionally whole, Ochberg created "The Color Wheel." The wheel is a circle divided like a pie into six pieces, much like in Trivial Pursuit, with each wedge a different color. Each color represents one of six positive emotions. For example, in his schema, yellow represents energy, the "feeling of exhilaration," or "jumping for joy, laughing out loud, having the wind in your hair while you are smiling all over."[24] Blue stands for "cool water and clear skies … for

---

[22]   Nagoski and Nagoski, *Burnout,* 213.
[23]   Ibid. at 214.
[24]   Ibid.

serenity, for calm, for relaxation, and ultimately, for bliss."[25] He recommends people go around the color wheel once a day to identify which color and corresponding set of emotions may be depleted, or missing, and focusing on thoughts and experiences that help to increase their sense of that color. As he's written: "By elevating the positive, you protect against the negative. You change your body chemistry in the right direction. You think about nourishing things in order to generate positive emotion. It takes time and practice, but it can alter the baseline of your being."[26]

Psychotherapist Wendy Kirk underscores the importance of giving yourself permission to feel joy. She explains how living a happy life, when we have the opportunity to do so, is a responsibility we have to ourselves and to each other. While we of course have an obligation to mitigate others' suffering, allowing guilt to paralyze us is counterproductive. She recently discussed Russia's invasion of Ukraine with an American woman who explained that she was having a hard time coping with everyday life, after regularly scouring the Internet for what was happening in the conflict and drowning in videos and photos that depicted the horror of the war. The woman explained that she was brushing her teeth when an enormous wave of guilt swept over her: "Who am I to have the privilege of brushing my teeth to go to bed, when so many people in Ukraine can't?"

Kirk countered, "What are people fighting so hard for, if not to have a life where they can brush their teeth and tuck their kids safely in at night? If no one is living that life, then that suggests there is nothing worth fighting for." Kirk says the more we are able to sustain healthy routines during times of conflict and stress the more stability and support we should feel. Structure is helpful when we experience chaos in our lives. Kirk also says we need to cultivate a deep appreciation for our own relative safety, while doing what we can to bear witness and support others.

Moreover, the guilt that arises from relative privilege – that is, I am taking my daughter to dance class in San Francisco while you are running from bombs in Kyiv – may prevent us from recognizing how we're being affected by trauma. The reality of our experience should not obscure pain that can be very real – whether we are literally in harm's way or suffering secondhand. That's not to equate the suffering (which would be offensive to those who are literally facing harm or death), but to recognize the disparate ways that violence and suffering affect us.

The generations of so-called digital natives, who have grown up with smartphones or iPads, sometimes literally since the crib, are facing a mental health crisis like never before. How technology and specifically social media come into play in health and well-being is the source of much research and analysis. Some

---

[25] Ibid.

[26] Joyce Boaz and Frank Ochberg. "PTSD Questions and Answers with Joyce Boaz and Dr. Frank Ochberg, M.D.: Gift from Within," available at: www.giftfromwithin.org/html/FAQ-Frank-Ochberg-Color-Wheel-of-Positive-Emotion.html (last visited July 16, 2022).

researchers are looking specifically at how institutions and especially schools can influence how adolescents take in social media – in more contextualized ways that foster agency and emphasize meaning and joy. For example, British psychologist Tom Harrison has looked at the potential to provide "education for online flourishing."[27] At the center of this research is the importance he sees in helping students build character in their approach to engaging with both humans and machines online.

Harrison and his colleagues at the Jubilee Centre for Character and Virtues promote a four-pronged approach to online engagement that could become the foundation for more formal education. Specifically, they believe that educators need to introduce students to cyber-wisdom literacy, reasoning, self-reflection, and motivation. Cyber-wisdom literacy is "the ability and language needed to identify different virtues online."[28] Cyber-wisdom reasoning requires fostering "the intellectual and critical ability to reflect on the best course of action online, particularly when presented with moral dilemmas and in ways that are dependent on context."[29] Cyber-wisdom self-reflection is "the practice of reflecting on one's own experiences online and of navigating, accordingly, the different perspectives and emotions involved in the process of making moral decisions online."[30] Finally, cyber-wisdom motivation requires developing a "subjective and a collective vision of the good life, as well as a motivation toward achieving human flourishing online."[31] Harrison puts all of this together within the overarching idea of "cyber-phronesis," the latter word meaning "practical wisdom" in ancient Greek.

So what does this look like *in practice* and how does it relate to cultivating meaning in our online lives? Consider twenty-two-year-old Will Mansson, who grew up in Sweden and moved to the United States to attend college at Penn State. Mansson has had a cell phone since he was about eight or nine years old, around the same time he got a computer. He said his parents, both psychologists, were pretty "checked out" when it came to technology. Mansson started out playing what he calls innocent Nintendo games and then moved to videogame staples like Call of Duty as well as to online social media spaces, including a now-defunct website called "LiveLeak."[32] On LiveLeak,[33] Mansson and his friends watched all kinds of

---

[27] Tom Harrison, "How You Can Help Kids Be Good People Online: Character Education Might Be the Key to a Better Internet and Help Kids Flourish Online, Suggests a Team of Researchers in the U.K.," *Greater Good Magazine*, January 27, 2022.

[28] Ibid.

[29] Ibid.

[30] Ibid.

[31] Ibid.

[32] James Vincent, "LiveLeak, the Internet's Font of Gore and Violence, Has Shut Down: After Fifteen Years in Operation, LiveLeak Is No More," *The Verge*, May 7, 2021.

[33] James Cook, "Q&A: The Man Behind LiveLeak, the Islamic State's Favorite Site for Beheading Videos," *Business Insider*, November 14, 2014. LiveLeak was launched by the same team that founded Ogrish.com, a site whose original tagline was "Can you handle life?"

violence, from people touching live power lines in Brazil to beheadings by ISIS to people being hit by cars. The site would pull from Closed-Circuit Television (CCTV) feeds to share the most graphic, violent content on the Internet.

Mansson was particularly affected by a video he saw when he was about sixteen years old that showed a young man having his throat slit by another. He says the details stick with him from this "very graphic violence that you have to be very broken inside to enjoy." Has this affected him emotionally? Mansson responded, "Do you mean has it made me numb?" He said it depends on the violence he's seeing. "Like I didn't mind – or at least half the time – I didn't mind seeing a person get run over. But if someone hits a dog, that's too much. So I'm very numb to one thing and very sensitive to another."

Sophie Mercer, a high-school student who has explored a wide array of websites since her first encounter with social media at the age of seven, has had a similar experience to Mansson. When asked whether she had ever encountered something online that she couldn't forget, she recalled an incident she had never shared with her parents. When she was twelve, she heard about a girl her age who livestreamed her suicide on a site where you could watch people kill themselves. Mercer was curious and visited the site. She explained that the "strange" thing was that "it wasn't the Livestream that got to me. It was the comments after that really upset me and I can't stop thinking about them." The comments sexualized the girl, including references to necrophilia. Commentators also derided the girl for her suicide, mocking her both for killing herself in a public place and for how she killed herself. The callousness with which people discussed the girl's death and the sarcastic posts that punctuated the livestream haunt Mercer years later. Like Mansson, she now has large variations in what affects her, with violence against people rarely sparking a reaction. "No matter how numb you are, though," Mercer explained, she knows "there's still damage done."

Mansson – who told us that he had spent nearly twenty-four hours on TikTok in the prior week, per the documentation on his smartphone – said that in spite of the amount of time he spends on social media, he does not derive any particular feelings of joy or meaning from that engagement. Mercer, who spends roughly twenty-eight hours a week on social media, said that she also doesn't find most sites pleasurable, because the content is largely "self-centered and meaningless." The exception is YouTube, she explained, because of a greater ability to engage with content that "has a purpose." She struggled to explain why she continues to spend so much time on the other sites – such as Instagram, TikTok, and Snapchat – despite the lack of pleasure or other meaning that she gets from that time online.

Thinking about cyber-phronesis in the context of Will Mansson's or Sophie Mercer's childhoods, we might imagine providing Will or Sophie with more tools – especially as young children – to think critically about the role and content of social media. Rather than just telling Will or Sophie to abstain from social media, they may have received more context for the violence they clicked on. They may have had more agency to determine if they should or should not view the material. They may have seen the events as the culmination of disparity or violence, for example, rather than as a one-off incident. We don't really know. But cultivating phronesis or cyber-wisdom in children – or simply cultivating awareness about information – may prepare them to view car crashes and other random disasters with more cautious, compassionate, and critical minds.

To complement kids' empowerment and education, there is, of course, also a need for regulation to minimize the types and quantity of graphic content they encounter online. LiveLeak shut down in 2021,[34] but access to an abundant assortment of disturbing content remains, including the site viewed by Mercer. Yet policy initiatives to curb access have largely failed. California is the first state to pass legislation that requires social media companies to consider the physical and mental health of young people in product design[35]; however, a similar bill that would have allowed government lawsuits against social media companies for causing harm or addiction in children failed. Social media companies – such as Meta and Snap – have aggressively opposed the legislation.[36] Time will tell whether California's requirement that companies consider kids' mental and physical well-being when designing their products results in net positive impact.

COLLECTIVE PURPOSE

Human rights investigator Sam Dubberley has always highlighted the meaning behind the often grueling labor of looking at graphic or hateful images. He's given his teams (whether journalists or human rights researchers or students) a *sense of purpose*: acknowledging that they aren't just looking at graphic, violent images for the sake of it, but rather to bring truth to light and to make change.

That sense of collective purpose and meaning is often harder to come by for content moderators. Contracted to review and take down problematic content for tech companies, they have noted that their work is largely individual and often lacks a collaborative or community underpinning within their companies. In a 2019 piece published in *The Verge* called "The Trauma Floor," Casey Newton blew the lid off the secondary trauma that contractors working with graphic content often experienced. One of the key takeaways expressed by the multiple people he interviewed was that they would look at terrible things all day but have no idea if the content they had singled out as offensive or in violation of the company's community guidelines

---

[34] James Vincent, "LiveLeak, the Internet's Font of Gore and Violence, Has Shut Down: After Fifteen Years in Operation, LiveLeak Is No More," *The Verge*, May 7, 2021.

[35] Christine Mai-Duc and Meghan Bobrowsky, "Social Media Companies Would Have to Consider Children's Health in Bill Passed by California Legislature," *Wall Street Journal*, August 20, 2022.

[36] Ibid. See also Meghan Bobrowsky, "California Gov. Gavin Newsom Signs Law Requiring Social Media Companies to Consider Children's Health," *Wall Street Journal*, September 15, 2022.

was actually taken down. One moderator said he found a horrible incident of abuse of an iguana by people who spoke Spanish and was told to send it to the "Spanish-speaking queue." He doubted there even was a Spanish-speaking queue and so he had watched this video – and was potentially traumatized by this video – without ever knowing if his work had any impact.

All of the researchers and content moderators we spoke with emphasized that what kept them going was a feeling of responsibility to *do* something in the face of wrongdoing. Mariana Jones,[37] a former content moderator, said, "I couldn't become blind to what was happening. I had a sense of responsibility. I wanted deeply to be able to figure out, 'What is this?'." She added that in spite of the grueling nature of her work, she would stay up late and work during off hours to make sure the content was taken down from the Internet or reported to child protective services, until the work began to consume her life. It wasn't until later that she realized this was a coping mechanism to deal with secondary trauma. AnaStacia Nicol Wright, the attorney who previously worked as a content moderator, agreed that finding meaning in and taking action related to her work of moderating sexual violence content made everything easier. "At some point it was like 'You know, we're helping these kids.'"

Adam Brown, from The New School for Social Research, Meg Satterthwaite of New York University School of Law, and Sarah Knuckey of Columbia University, along with their colleagues, conducted 110 interviews with advocates and experts from 35 countries to understand how those in the human rights field – be they journalists, advocates, lawyers, or other types of researchers – react to working with upsetting materials day in and day out.[38] Their study emphasizes that looking at distressing content isn't as distressing or potentially traumatizing if it's done for a reason – that is, taking action to stop violence or suffering in some way.

The massive public response to George Floyd's murder is a perfect example of the human urge to make meaning from distressing content and to *do something* that has impact or brings the work to a broader community and conversation – something that is known to have a protective effect. Brown noted that videos that have stirred public action, such as the video of George Floyd's murder, can be traumatizing, while also making us feel like we're part of a bigger movement. In fact, the sense of connection and agency derived from collective outrage can mitigate the personal distress experienced in encountering the content. He cited a study from Turkey that showed that protesters thrown into prison together had a lower incidence of PTSD than people who were randomly incarcerated. In referencing the Turkey study,

---

[37] We use a pseudonym for Mariana throughout this book given the sensitive nature of what she revealed.

[38] Margaret Satterthwaite, Sarah Knuckey, Ria Singh Sawhney, Katie Wightman, Rohini Bagrodia, and Adam Brown, "Trauma, Depression, and Burnout in the Human Rights Field: Identifying Barriers to Resilient Advocacy," 49 *Columbia Human Rights Law Review* 267 (2018).

Brown said the "cognitive orientation" of those collectively engaged in a movement can be more positive than that of those who experience difficult phenomena on their own.

Brown's research collaborator, Meg Satterthwaite, emphasized that white people were catalyzed in new ways by the George Floyd video. "I have heard a lot of Black people say it was retraumatizing to see [the video], hear about it, be talked to about it and that it was again a spectacle, but the catalyzing nature was a way of acting out of power instead of being disempowered," she said. "If you can find some way to reconnect with action, take action, and have an efficacy in the world and can make things better, then if you can join with other people and take a step to stop it? It's not only going to help society but will help people [as] individuals."

Sometimes the action we take may not be the kind of purposeful, collective action that mitigates secondary trauma. There is interesting research, for example, that looks at one way in which many of us use social media, namely to "vent," that is, express strong emotions about something that's upset us, and whether the short term "feel good" effects of venting have positive long-term impact. At least one randomized, controlled study found that venting about a traumatic experience was not helpful for alleviating distress because it kept that trauma salient.[39] Another study, which looked at how students vented in the aftermath of 9/11, similarly found that those who vented "suffered from more anxiety up to four months later than those who didn't," and that the students' "focus on and venting of emotions was found to be uniquely predictive of longer-term anxiety."[40] Of course, this may be merely correlative, not causative, meaning that there may be other reasons than the students' focus for heightened anxiety. Yet another study analyzed the effects on students of venting on social media after school shootings at two universities. They found that "while students thought that venting was beneficial, their post-traumatic stress and depression scores actually went up the more they vented."[41]

Author Jill Suttie of UC Berkeley's Greater Good Science Center is one of the researchers who has urged caution about venting on the Internet. As she explains, "while sharing our emotions online can help us feel better in the moment and identify supportive allies, results can be mixed. For one thing, negative emotions easily spread online, which may create a herd mentality, resulting in bullying or trolling – especially if you identify a particular person as responsible for your feelings."[42]

---

[39] M. Sijbrandij, M. Olff, J. B. Reitsma, I. V. Carlier, and B. P. Gersons, "Emotional or Educational Debriefing after Psychological Trauma. Randomised Controlled Trial," 189 *British Journal of Psychiatry* 150 (2006).

[40] Gabrielle I. Liverant, Stefan G. Hofmann, and Brett T. Litz, "Coping and Anxiety in College Students after the September 11th Terrorist Attacks," 17 *Anxiety, Stress and Coping* 127 (2004).

[41] Jill Suttie, "Does Venting Your Feelings Actually Help?" *Greater Good Magazine*, June 21, 2021.

[42] Ibid.

Other scholars have found that the venting we do may not hurt us but *may* negatively affect our followers and other online audiences who read or watch the content we post. As reported in *Greater Good Magazine*, "being around someone stuck in anger, fear, or sadness cycles can be overwhelming for listeners who may end up 'catching' the emotions themselves," and can ultimately strain social relationships. There's also the danger that once we are exposed to something upsetting, like what Will Mansson expressed, we won't be able to get it out of our minds.

Fortunately, researchers have identified some helpful methods for those who find themselves ruminating on an upsetting post. For example, the UC Berkeley neuroscientist Ronald Dahl explains the value of switching attention to something competing, which has equivalent or greater emotional weight than the upsetting content. He describes a body of work that explores the power of "savoring." Savoring is the "mirror image" of worry and rumination: not simply casually calling to mind something positive that has happened in your life but remembering it with all of your senses. Dana McMakin, now on the faculty at Florida International University, experimented with a series of "savoring interventions," originally aimed at eight- to thirteen-year olds. The children would identify a positive memory during the daytime that they'd like to return to when worried. They would replay the memory, remembering the sights, sounds, feelings, and smells that accompanied its formation. The children were asked to think of their brain as a television or YouTube site and then develop a series of savored memories that they would add to their "savoring channel." They would then practice flipping between their "worrying channel," where upsetting memories lived, acknowledge that "watching" that worrying channel was normal, and then practice flipping to their savoring channel. This would give them clinical scaffolding for self-soothing and gaining greater agency over their emotions. Studies like these, Dahl says, are indicative of an important point: that you can't just push away the negative and that the positive rarely feels as salient. Switching takes practice.

Dahl also explains that there's another cognitive piece that can be layered on top of the savoring: namely, influencing the narrative that one constructs around an experience. In our work with students conducting digital human rights investigations, we found this to be an important aspect of cultivating resilience. We encouraged students and gave them time to learn about the politics, culture, and daily lives of people in Syria, Myanmar, and Hong Kong who had otherwise been reduced to the subjects of violent or distressing videos. The context – the surrounding narrative – became hugely important in helping to navigate the tragedy in the images and in providing meaning for the work.

That brings us back to the venting process. According to psychologist Ethan Kross, author of the book *Chatter*, there are relatively healthy ways to vent that can also help with disrupting ruminations and support the reframing of an experience. Kross recommends that instead of venting in isolation, you seek out perspective from your online audiences. This engagement can help interrupt the rumination cycle by bringing in new perspectives and reframing what a situation means, including what's possible as a response.

Social media users can also choose to approach a targeted few with whom to vent as opposed to a general audience, looking for those who will help process the experience and may provide especially helpful suggestions for how to turn negative emotions into actions and greater understanding. Kross also recommends writing down or meditating about particular thoughts, instead of merely amplifying them on social media. Individuals may also want to change their environment (for example, going outside if inside, or taking a shower) to interrupt ruminations and support emotion processing.

Kross ultimately comes down on the side of thinking that venting *can* result in a net good if done strategically, helping people to cope with distress – and that if social media posters can move beyond just letting off steam to some kind of productive action, they can end up in a place where they not only feel better but have strengthened relationships. As he's explained, "Venting serves some function. It has benefits for the self in terms of satisfying our social and emotional needs. We just need to find out what the correct venting dosage is and make sure to offer to supplement that with cognitive reframing."[43]

According to several researchers, then, social media use can have both negative and positive effects. Social media use is at its most negative when it reduces face-to-face interactions, detracts from meaningful communication, and leaves people "depressed, anxious and lonely."[44] But positive effects can include the ability to offer "a valuable outlet for expression and social sharing."[45] For example, people who struggle to communicate verbally in social interactions may find that communication through social media is far less stressful than face-to-face interactions and may be a mechanism that strengthens meaningful connection.[46] In one study, researchers Eva Buechel and Jonah Berger analyzed the impact of "microblogging" on well-being. Microblogging includes communications via social media that are disseminated to no specific person, such as public-facing tweets and Facebook posts. Buechel and Berger found such interactions especially helpful to people with social apprehension who have a hard time with direct engagement, but (like all humans) crave and need social interaction. Importantly, as pointed out by the authors, most social media sites offer multiple ways to communicate, whether through posts, direct messaging, live streaming, or otherwise, providing individuals with a diverse array of options for connection.[47]

---

[43] Suttie, "Does Venting Your Feelings Actually Help?" (quoting Kross).
[44] E. C. Buechel and J. Berger, "Microblogging and the Value of Undirected Communication," 28 *Journal of Consumer Psychology* 40 (2018) (citing Kraut et al 1998, Tonioni et al 2012, and Turkle, 2015).
[45] Ibid.
[46] Ibid.
[47] Ibid.

Many of the people with whom we spoke underscored the urgent need to better understand, research, and amplify the positives of social media, even while acknowledging and addressing the harms. When asked if there were positives to social media, Liz Scott – the social media content moderator – smiled. "I really like TikTok. I did my hair in cat ears [because of TikTok]. It sounds weird, maybe it's just the algorithm. ... It's sparked creativity. I think anything that inspires people to be more creative [is healthy]. And that's what I focus on. Something to get my thoughts back." For Scott, regaining who you used to be when you're robbed of yourself by your near-constant exposure to graphic online material comes, in part, through creativity, through remembering what brings you joy.

However, not all platforms are the same in their ability to connect us with something meaningful. We tend to treat social media platforms as monolithic, but they're not. They engage users in different ways and optimize for different things. How might they – and we, through our use of these sites – optimize for creativity and connection? In addition, we may find ourselves in very different "corners" of social media sites based on our demographics. Whereas Scott felt that TikTok was a more positive place for her to spend time online than, say, YouTube or Facebook, two teenagers with whom we spoke felt differently, describing YouTube as helpful for research, connection, and learning, but TikTok as "toxic." Regardless, when our online experiences start to leave us feeling drained instead of energized and inspired, it may be helpful to shift platforms, audiences, and online communities.

When discussing how to create more positive outcomes from our online engagement, Mariana Jones, the former content moderator, was thoughtful: "Education and awareness are really critical: How [the information] is consumed." Equally important to learning how to assess the quality of the information is what to do with problematic content you do come across, in order to improve the experiences of others: "Do you report this? Where? Where do you go? That also gives the person some agency, which we want. We all want to help, especially when we see someone in pain."

Jones noted that her work in online trust and safety has generated not just her most painful moments but also her proudest. She says closure in the form of human connection helps people transition – "whether it's like a hug or whether it's just like eye connection." She said that when you are just consuming the content without this connection, it's like "you have a tube in your throat and you're just being [constantly] fed this content, and you don't get that type of closure. The thing that hurts me the most is the lack of closure."

Jones's perspective from the frontlines of content moderation and almost exclusively within the online, digital world, is strangely similar to that of boots-on-the-ground investigator Stover. While Stover always emphasizes that you can never truly find closure after surviving a human rights violation or losing a loved one, you can find some healing through knowing – knowing the facts and circumstances surrounding their disappearance, even of something unthinkable. And that knowing can lead us to some sense of purpose and meaning as we view and attend to pain in our communities and in our world.

TAKEAWAYS

What, then, are some of the ways in which we can move from defending ourselves against mental distress, to fostering meaning, happiness, empathy, and other positive emotions? Below are activities that may help.

Build up your resilience to provide a foundation for positive emotions: As noted by the founders of RatedR, "You can't pour from an empty cup." Our capacity to help others comes from helping, respecting, and honoring ourselves. This means ensuring we provide ourselves with self-care, the common analogy being donning our oxygen masks on an airplane before turning to assist our child. This could mean assessing how well you are conducting self-care, which includes the basics of having showered, drunk water, and eaten. As the RatedR founders underscore, "This is [critical] because our mental wellbeing is tied to our physical wellbeing. When we feel good physically, we can feel good mentally."[48] And as Audre Lorde, the American poet and civil rights activist has declared, "Caring for [one]self is not self-indulgence, it is self-preservation, and that is an act of political warfare."

Practice savoring: The neuroscientist and pediatrician Ronald Dahl recommends "savoring" some competing thing – not only remembering something positive (like eating a super ripe peach) but remembering it with all of your senses (the nectar-like smell, the feel of sticky juice and textured skin, the slurp of each bite). Create a bank of savoring images in your mind to return to if you begin ruminating on a distressing video or photograph.[49]

Experience and express empathy: Recognize the sadness and trauma you're taking in when you read news or watch online content and acknowledge the feelings that come up. We may not be able to express feelings of empathy to someone who has been directly affected, but we can share that sense of empathy with our loved ones and colleagues.

Vent, but vent thoughtfully and strategically: Venting can have negative effects for you and your various audiences, if you're just sending negative emotions into the world. But if you vent strategically – to colleagues or other audiences online who may help you reframe your thinking or help you identify pathways to action – that venting becomes purposeful and tethered to the meaning and purpose that we know have strong protective effects.

---

[48] Rachael Cornejo and Lili Siri Spira, "Beyond Burnout: Hacking Your Way to a Better Work-Life Balance," The Diana Initiative, July 21, 2021, available at: www.youtube.com/watch?v=ypWMGr2u6SE (last visited July 14, 2022).

[49] Ira Newman, Jeremy Adam Smith, Jull Suttie, and Maryam Abdullah, "The Top 10 Insights from 'A Science of Meaningful Life' in 2021" *Greater Good Science Center*, December 16, 2021.

Balance out your time online by using all of your senses – especially touch: Neuroscientists say that touch is a fundamental element of human connection – an element that is of course missing from online interactions. Even elbow bumps in an era of heightened fear about physical connection, for instance, can serve the purpose.

Use the color wheel to identify and encourage expression of positive emotions you're missing: Use Ochberg's color wheel to take stock and build awareness about your reactions to news or social media and find ways to return all of the colors of the world to your life, bringing them into balance.

Breathe and be mindful: A practice of breathing or mindfulness doesn't need to be time-consuming or elaborate. Research shows that first responders (fire-fighters, police officers, and social workers), all benefit from a mindfulness practice. What could this look like? This could mean taking five minutes a day with your feet planted on the floor, taking ten breaths in through your nose and out through your mouth. It could be imagining sunlight flooding into your body, from the top of your head to the bottom of your feet. It could also mean a walk (without your phone) where you try to take in every tree and leaf or every sign post and front door. Mindfulness can also be practiced with someone else, in the case of active listening.

Connect with those who are affected: In digital spaces, as pointed out in the introduction to this chapter, we do not have the same means of connecting with those who are affected by violence as people who are in physical proximity, like Eric Stover and his team on the ground in Guatemala, working directly with the families of the disappeared. If physical contact isn't possible, another way to connect is by exploring the full richness and complexity of the people who have been most affected. In our Investigations Lab, we encouraged teams of students to find ways to expand their lens beyond investigating the violence in, say, a war zone, to see a fuller human picture of the people and culture – the food, language, art, and poetry – underscoring how important it is to see the positive aspects of a society, not just the negative. This critical human element – life and joy, as discussed above – was always integral to the journalist's or human rights investigator's experience on the ground in an international context. In a digital world, it's harder to achieve and thus we need to be even more intentional about making it happen.

Find meaning, make impact: Rather than mindlessly taking in graphic content and letting it wash over us in ways that make us feel impotent, find ways to make meaning from what you've seen. Of course, this can't be done with every piece of graphic content we take in. Building off the previous takeaway, just the act of doing *something* can mitigate our feelings of powerlessness. If we're distressed by watching videos of police brutality, for example, we may be able to find ways to volunteer with or donate to community-based organizations challenging racism or police abuse. If we're troubled by the hate targeting immigrants and the barrage of online hate speech directed at these communities, we can find a way to volunteer or give funds or goods to refugees and immigrants in need in our community.

Collective action, like collective grief, can be a powerful antidote to the pain and heaviness of the world.

Ultimately, all of our news viewing can be about meaning-making and a sense of empowerment and purpose that can strengthen not only our ability to function but also make room for the introduction of more positive emotions – a deeper sense of truth, awe at the courage of others, and joy in collective action for a better world.

Share a good laugh: Gallows humor, also known as dark humor, has always been a means for coping with intense experiences – whether in a newsroom or operating room, or on a battlefront. Researchers say laughter can be a psychological and even physiological release following a traumatic event.[50] Whether by binge watching a light-hearted show, taking in a romantic comedy, or streaming TikToks of cat life, humor can bolster our resiliency by acting as a valve for safely blowing off steam.

---

[50] Heather S. Lonczak, "Humor in Psychology: Coping and Laughing Your Woes Away," *Positive Psychology*, July 8, 2020.

7

Policy and Practice

What Next?

On March 15, 2019, a young man opened fire in Christchurch, New Zealand, just outside the Al Noor Mosque. Within minutes, dozens of people – most of Muslim faith – were dead or dying. The man quickly moved on to a second site, the Linwood Islamic Center, where just fifteen minutes later, he once again opened fire. Altogether, fifty-one people were murdered, another forty-nine seriously injured.[1]

Like many violent extremists, the perpetrator had promoted his plans on websites known for fomenting real-world violence and goading individuals into committing horrific acts that would earn them "infamy."[2] Particularly insidious in this case, however, was that he live-streamed the first attack on Facebook, bringing the killings into homes across the globe *as they happened*. "Content moderators" at Facebook, Twitter, YouTube, and other social media sites flew to their "war rooms" – the spaces they use to respond to tragedies as they unfold on their sites – to try to remove the horrors playing out across the Internet. They were ill equipped to stem the hemorrhaging. Within minutes, the live stream, in millions of permutations, had begun flooding the Internet, the versions too diverse for algorithms to effectively detect and delete.[3]

Unfortunately, the killer's harm endured long after his killing spree. From the families of those murdered, to content moderators charged with locating and taking down the footage across multiple online sites, to the merely curious, the horrors of that morning resonated long after the live streamer was physically detained. At least two people – the killer's uncounted casualties – would allegedly commit suicide after watching the graphic footage.

---

[1] Rosie Perper, Kieran Corcoran, and Michelle Mark, "51 People Were Killed and 49 Others Were Injured after a Gunman Opened Fire at Two Mosques in Christchurch, New Zealand," *The Insider*, March 15, 2019.

[2] Washington Post, "Inside YouTube's Struggle to Shut Down Video of the New Zealand Shooting – and the Humans Who Outsmarted Its Systems," March 18, 2019.

[3] Ibid.

Since that horrific day, companies and governments have rallied to better address the viral spread of what they label "terrorist" content, and in the process, have shown what might be possible with other graphic posts, specifically how they might be detected, removed from public view, and then preserved for later justice and accountability. In this chapter, we offer a number of recommendations for those who are in a position to do something technically, structurally, legally, or otherwise to minimize the risk of harm that comes with disturbing material online. While space limitations constrict how deep we can go into policy issues and recommendations (which would require *several* books), we strongly recommend existing seminal work on these topics.[4] In the meantime, in this chapter, we tease out the policy implications of what our interviewees shared and lay out a series of recommendations for companies, governments, and individuals.

COMPETING INTERESTS OF SOCIAL MEDIA COMPANIES

An important place to start is by thinking about the worlds we enter when we go online – and what dictates what we find when we get there. Social media companies juggle numerous and sometimes competing interests when deciding what content to keep up, what to take down, what to promote, and whether to attach content warnings or other labels to posts deemed problematic.[5] These interests have a significant impact on corporate policies *and* government responses.

One of the first of these interests is of course a financial one – how to keep people viewing content on platforms in order to serve up more potential customers for advertisers. This tends to weigh in favor of keeping up salacious content, which is known to attract more attention than less controversial posts.

The second interest is the international human right to freedom of expression, which in the United States has its closest domestic parallel in a commitment to free speech as established by the US Constitution's First Amendment. Freedom of expression has long been recognized as a human right, critical to the healthy functioning of democracies by allowing diverse perspectives to inform social behavior and allowing anyone to challenge the narratives and opinions of people in power. Freedom of expression, as an interest, also weighs in favor of platforms keeping even controversial material up and has been a driving force behind content moderation

---

[4] These include Safiya Noble's 2018 book, *Algorithms of Oppression,* which addresses the ways in which racism and misogyny are replicated and even amplified by algorithms that affect what we see online; Sarah Roberts' 2019 book *Behind the Screen,* which documents the experiences of content moderators; and David Kaye's 2020 book, *Speech Police,* on technology, human rights and competing policy interests, among others.

[5] David Kaye, *Speech Police: The Global Struggle to Govern the Internet* (Columbia Global Reports 2019); Alexa Koenig, Shakiba Mashayekhi, Diana Chavez-Varela, Lindsay Freeman, Kayla Brown, Zuzanna Buszman, et al, *Digital Lockers: Archiving Social Media Evidence of Atrocity Crimes* (Human Rights Center 2021).

policies in the United States. Indeed, many social media platforms promote their sites as spaces for people to speak with minimal fear of censorship.

Although people in the United States often talk about freedom of expression as a First Amendment issue, there are two problems with using the latter terminology to discuss what circulates – and what should circulate – online. First, this concept is uniquely American since it is based on the US Constitution and therefore isn't applicable to much of the world. Second, the Constitution puts limits on *government* action, not on the actions of private corporations, which have the right to determine for themselves what they allow and don't allow on their sites (with a few exceptions for material that is prohibited by law, like child sexual exploitation). Thus, the First Amendment isn't relevant to what stays up and what comes down from private "social" spaces, even though the human right to *freedom of expression* is relevant.

A third, related interest is the human right of access to information, which focuses less on the person who does the posting, and more on the recipient. Making sure people can access helpful or other quality information also mitigates in favor of letting even graphic content remain online, especially when there's a social interest in the material.

Unlike these first three interests, a fourth – national security – often weighs in favor of taking content down. Content that implicates this interest may include, for example, posts that incite people to riot, recruit people into dangerous organizations, or leak top-secret or other confidential information.

A fifth major interest is privacy. Although social media is especially infamous for the lack of privacy it often engenders, privacy interests also usually weigh in favor of takedowns. Privacy interests may be held by the person who posted the material, those depicted in the material, or others affected by its dissemination. Doxxing – the malicious sharing of private information, such as a despised politician's home address accompanied by calls to harass or intimidate them, or the posting of a hacked or leaked video that shows someone in a compromising situation or an intimate moment – is just one example of the many types of posts that might be removed for privacy reasons. Privacy is also the reason social media companies often give when refusing to share information with third parties, such as researchers or law enforcement.

As for what goes up and what stays up, each company crafts its own terms of use and community guidelines, which are the "rules" by which users are expected to abide by when circulating information on the company's site. Companies' rules are often designed to balance the interests outlined above, even if they sometimes favor one interest more than the others. Internal policy documents provide additional guidance for the companies' employees and contractors, who have to decide what to do with potentially problematic content, specifically whether it violates the companies' rules of engagement, and if not, whether new rules are needed. For example, while all major social media platforms remove terrorist content, what is considered "terrorist" differs between Facebook and YouTube, and Twitter and TikTok.

When these rules and policies prove deficient for meeting various pro-social aims, like protecting people from harmful content, approaches for countering the harms can be roughly clustered into individual, cultural, and structural interventions. Individual approaches include what people can do to protect themselves. Cultural approaches focus on norm setting about what is good versus what is bad, what is forbidden versus permitted. Structural approaches can include everything from new laws that dictate what options are available to companies, governments, and the public, to corporate workflows, to the algorithms that affect what we see in our feeds (literally, what we are "fed" online, which in turn affects our digital, physical, and social well-being). This last category includes warnings and click throughs that some companies have begun to attach to graphic or otherwise disturbing posts, which are designed to make the viewer more conscious about what they choose to view, share, or amplify and technical interventions like blurring potentially upsetting content or information that violates privacy interests (such as peoples' faces or license plates).

Ultimately, even if all of us, regardless of age, do our best to thrive in digital spaces, and companies continue to devise new interventions to minimize our exposure to graphic content, algorithms devised by social media platforms are pitted against us. Those algorithms are designed to ensure we spend as much time as possible on the platforms by feeding us the content they think will most keep us glued to our screens, which is often the most shocking content, not necessarily the most informational or uplifting. In this way, companies maximize user time on screen, which is a metric that advertisers use in determining where to put their money. The British researcher Harrison explains:

> This is when what might be called *education for online flourishing* gets tricky. From the outset, it is important to state that it is so tricky because of the actions of many of the companies that run social media platforms and other apps that use the Internet. So many of the big players have seemingly prioritized (despite their rhetoric) market value over human values. They have designed new playgrounds for our children that, because of limited government regulation or self-regulation, are often minefields full of moral obstacles.[6]

Researchers affiliated with George Washington University have extensively studied how algorithms affect what we see, increasing our exposure to potentially harmful online information.[7] They analyzed a massive data set, investigating public behavior on 500 Facebook pages that receive the most engagement from users, in order

---

[6] Tom Harrison, "How You Can Help Kids Be Good People Online: Character Education Might Be the Key to a Better Internet and Help Kids Flourish Online, Suggests a Team of Researchers in the U.K.," *Greater Good Magazine*, January 27, 2022, available at: https://greatergood.berkeley.edu/article/item/how_you_can_help_kids_be_good_people_online.

[7] Matthew Hindman, Nathaniel Lubin, and Trevor Davis, "Facebook Has a Superuser-Supremacy Problem," *The Atlantic*, February 10, 2022.

to better understand how people spread hate and misinformation on the platform, and how the platform's actions affect that behavior. What they found was that a small handful of negative super-users are "hyper influential," and "part of an elite, previously unreported class of users that produce more likes, shares, reactions, comments, and posts than 99 percent of Facebook users in America."[8] They warn that "because Facebook's algorithms reward engagement, these superusers have enormous influence over which posts are seen first in other users' feeds, and which are never seen at all." Of the 52 million active users on US pages and public groups, "the top 1 percent of accounts were responsible for 35 percent of all observed interactions; the top 3 percent were responsible for 52 percent."[9]

This has huge implications for policy and what needs to be done to clean up our now toxic virtual playgrounds, including what regulations may help in minimizing harm. One of their most important findings is how the dominance of superusers affects something Facebook calls "Meaningful Social Interaction" ("MSI") or what Mark Zuckerberg describes as "connecting with people we care about."[10] Posts are scored for their MSI value, with different points assigned for likes versus anger versus comments. Tweaking the points value for each of these can radically influence what kinds of content makes it into our feeds – as well as the toxicity of those materials.

Since content that drives a strong, emotive reaction often receives the most points, potentially upsetting content is most likely to dominate our feeds – and that of our kids. Analogizing to the physical world, Harrison explains a related challenge for parents:

> Many of us simply do not know what our children are doing [or are exposed to] online; it's somewhat of a black box. For example, whereas it was easy to spot aggression in the playground, it is much harder to know if our children are subjected to (or perpetrating) bullying on platforms like Snapchat. Second, rules online are different: Children can transcend time and space in a way I never could when I grew up. If I wanted to speak to a friend, I had to hang around on the street until one came along, call them on a tethered landline, or wait until I saw them in school. In the age of TikTok, Snapchat, and Instagram, this is not the case; it's not uncommon for children to have thousands of micro-interactions with their friends ... all day and night. Those affordances alone don't mean that children will necessarily behave un-virtuously online, but they have changed the rules of engagement. When children think they can act anonymously and in ways that are largely unrestricted, then it is perhaps not surprising that worrying Internet trends like harmful TikTok challenges spring up, where children are encouraged to commit shocking actions, such as messing up school signs or smacking a teacher.

[8] Ibid.
[9] Ibid.
[10] Matthew Hindman, Nathaniel Lubin, and Trevor Davis, "Facebook Has a Superuser-Supremacy Problem," *The Atlantic*, February 10, 2022.

Given this context, as well as the findings earlier in this book, we offer the following feedback below: suggestions for improving social media company employees' online experiences; suggestions for improving users' online experiences; and suggestions for building our future online worlds in ways that minimize the risks of psychosocial harm from potentially "dangerous" content and maximize the potential benefits.

IMPROVING CONTENT MODERATORS' EXPERIENCES

Emiliana Simon-Thomas, science director of UC Berkeley's Greater Good Science Center, has long advised social media companies about their internal operations and has spent quite a bit of time thinking about the experiences of employees who are regularly exposed to graphic content. These people range from content moderators, otherwise known as the "cleaners" of the Internet,[11] to trust and safety officers who may find and feed what they believe are dangerous posts to law enforcement. Simon-Thomas has a doctorate in Cognition Brain and Behavior from Berkeley and focused her dissertation on unpleasant emotions' impact on decision-making. When asked her thoughts on how to minimize the risks that come with exposure to graphic content and what that might suggest for everyday users, Simon-Thomas' recommendations ranged from providing employees with greater control over their working conditions to limiting the hours of exposure. "[Content moderation] can't be someone's full time job. There *has* to be a tap out," she said. She warned that the negative ramifications of this work can be long-lasting: "People know when they're about to go over the edge and start numbing themselves. That doesn't limit itself to the workplace. That kind of [trauma and response] will affect their entire life."

Liz Scott, who formerly supervised content moderators at YouTube, has similarly grappled with how to minimize exposure to harm.

> "I remember when we organized the first team that focused on child sexual abuse. We ensured they wouldn't work a full eight hours. They would get paid for eight hours, but not work the entire time. We also pulled people together into a large office to work together for some camaraderie, and also to have a space where they could go to do this work and then be able to leave the space. Then have a psychologist come in to help and support them." What especially upset her was that moderators' labor was so little valued; they were being exposed to the most toxic things people do to each other, yet not granted a living wage, decent benefits, or stability by their employers. She argued for greater compensation for the workers, as well as greater job security to foster their sense of belonging. "Mostly I was like 'man, content moderators need a union.'"

What is less known than the potential harms that can accrue from heavy exposure to toxic online content is the extent to which those harms might last. Mariana Jones,[12]

[11]   PBS, *The Cleaners*, available at: www.pbs.org/independentlens/documentaries/the-cleaners/.
[12]   A pseudonym.

who has worked in trust and safety for two of the world's largest social media platforms but has since changed roles to work on the ethical issues implicated by new technologies, said that even as this work recedes in her rearview mirror, the horrors she witnessed linger. "Lucky me, I left. I have the resources. But I will probably have PTSD for the rest of my life."

Given the lingering effects of the work, Jones stressed the importance of companies paying attention to not just the short- but also the long-term well-being of the people doing this work. "Should companies have a responsibility to check in with people months after they finish? I was fortunate because my manager came from a trust and safety background. But I think that's an area where there could be more improvement. Maybe an exit program or extra time for your transition [from content-based work to other work]? Something like, as part of your exit package, we're going to pay for a month or two for you to reset and re-incorporate yourself into 'normal' society."

In addition to thinking about what happens to people when they leave their employment, companies also need to pay attention to how employees and contractors enter *into* the work. Being an employee of a company – not just a contractor – matters for having a sense of inclusion and belonging. And companies need to recognize the disparate working conditions and engage only contractors who address the mental health conditions of their employees. Watching hours of graphic footage and making difficult calls about whether something stays up or comes down and whether it is reposted to law enforcement isn't rote or menial labor. How can companies ensure adequate benefits and compensation, job security, and the sense of community needed by *all* people doing this work?

Moreover, as discussed in Chapter 4, research indicates that being prepared for and not surprised by difficult content is absolutely essential to mitigating secondary trauma. And yet many of the current or former content moderators who spoke with us indicated that they didn't have any real idea of the content they would be monitoring until their first days on the job – and had no training or other preparation before beginning work.

Scott, who formerly worked for YouTube and its parent company, Google, spoke to some of the reasons for this lack of preparation, including the companies' sometimes rapidly changing priorities around what stays up and what comes down, which is driven in part by erupting emergencies and in part by politics, and how that can dictate sudden changes in staffing that leave personnel vulnerable. "There are so many pressures in the [content moderation] space. ... Those pressures shift with the winds and moment. All of a sudden [after a highly publicized terror attack] an exec said we need to hire 10,000 people" to remove terrorism-related posts. "Some people working on Google books were then reorganized into content moderation" and reassigned to that effort. She noted that they had very little preparation for what they were about to work on, which was a radical change from the kinds of tasks they'd been hired to do. She noted this experience was one of a "handful of reasons" that she ultimately left her job: "I had become a manager and I had become responsible for a lot of the relationships, for the contractors and stuff, and since people were just being [reassigned] from Google books, I thought that that was really wrong. When [the employees] asked me will I have access to a psychologist [once I start this work] I had to say 'I don't know.'" But she struggled with how to better respond to these sudden shifts in need. "Structurally, how do you avoid that situation? Fall back on automation?"

Automation is one possible response, and one that could go a long way toward minimizing human harms. As technologist Ashley Bradford's work has demonstrated, it is possible to develop algorithms that can be trained to automatically detect various kinds of graphic content – such as blood or beheadings – and provide warnings to potential viewers, or create an overlay that allows for automatic blurring or desyncing of visuals and sound that can be turned off if needed or desired. But companies have yet to prioritize such features. So far, even war crimes and human rights investigators have mostly chosen to deploy automatic image detection and natural language processing to help identify and increase access to the most relevant content for their investigations, yet have failed to think through how that same technology can be used to protect their teams and give them greater options and thus control over what they see, how they see it, and when.

Until such time as widespread automation takes place, general working conditions of course matter, as does making sure managers and other higher-ups are aware of what you're exposed to and recognize that they need to care about its effect. Scott underscored the power that corporate leaders have to improve those conditions, noting their ability to build worker protections into their contracts with external organizations. "There was a contract that Google had [with a foreign company] that I heard about. One of the [team members] working abroad had allegedly seen that all of the women were making less than the men. Google leaders saw it and decided to renegotiate. With one swoop of a pen, those people got more. [But changes like that currently] fall on the goodness of someone's heart." Instead, a commitment to worker protection must be baked into corporate policy and practice, as well as the broader corporate ethos.

Both Simon-Thomas and Jones stressed how important it was for companies to empower content moderators to develop greater awareness of the interventions over which they have control, as well as to better understand the positive impacts that have resulted from their efforts. Simon-Thomas recommended that companies help employees "focus on and understand how they are doing something that really matters to people, finding ways to bring that in" to the work. We also spoke with trust and safety officers – social media company employees whose job it is to police content on websites and keep users safe – who stressed their deep hunger to know what happened with posts they shared with law enforcement or reported to the National Center for Missing and Exploited Children (NCMEC): Were prosecutions brought? Was a child saved? Or did their documentation and reporting fall into some deep, dark pit?

Lack of knowledge about what happened to the humans or animals that the content moderators and safety officers struggled to save is a huge part of what haunts and what hurts. One possible remedy would be for companies to hire outside researchers to explore the outcomes of various cases, pulling together information from those doing the work with feedback from outside organizations and individuals, such as NCMEC or the police. Another would be to integrate feedback – not just quantitative but qualitative – into work flows and processes, such as setting up report-back mechanisms. Similarly, news organizations that report on traumatic events can do a better job circling back with readers to report outcomes of efforts to hold people accountable or even just on the well-being of those who were harmed.

Access to therapy for content moderators – or for anyone affected by online content – can also help. Ideally, there are multiple pathways into psychological support, whether from a therapist on staff to mental health coverage to peer counseling. The people we spoke with who had worked as content moderators, as reporters, or as human rights researchers were profoundly impacted by their work. In their exposure to digital documentation of atrocities, they were exposed to a variety and depth of cruelty that most people never encounter. Several of those we interviewed did have positive things to say about their employers and the resources they were given in terms of therapy, connection, and more. For those working at a social media company, that mostly came from people who had transitioned from temporary work to permanent employment. They remarked on the protective effect of the additional resources that came with their more secure status, both in terms of access to resources (like therapy, paid leave, and limited hours) and stronger psychological connections to their colleagues and the organizations for which they work, including a better sense of inclusion and belonging.

Once in therapy, it's critical for the participant to commit to it. Jones explained that while she had been lucky to have access to a therapist through her work with social media platforms, "It wasn't until two years ago that I started to take therapy religiously, seriously, going every week. Really talking about [what I was experiencing]." That said, companies shouldn't offer an insufficient handful of counseling sessions as a means of relinquishing responsibility for the potential harms to content moderators. This should be just one offering, one tool in the tool box for mitigating secondary trauma.

A number of lawsuits filed against the social media platforms seek to compel such changes. As just one example, in May 2020, Facebook settled a class action lawsuit brought by a number of content moderators who alleged they had been harmed from viewing graphic content while performing services for Facebook through a vendor called PRO Unlimited.[13] The plaintiffs claimed that they were suffering from

---

[13] Content moderators were defined in the settlement agreement as "any individual who works in a group that reviews user-generated content posted to Facebook platforms to determine whether, or to train Artificial Intelligence to determine whether, such material violates Facebook's Community Standards." Scola v. Facebook, Inc., Superior Court of the State of California, County of San Mateo Case No. 18-civ-05135 (2021) (Final Approval of Settlement).

significant psychological trauma and PTSD, with symptoms ranging from insomnia to fatigue to social anxiety.[14] The lawsuit produced more than 500,000 pages of discovery – the background information, testimony, data, and other potential evidence related to the case. The class extended to all content moderators who worked for Facebook in California, Arizona, Texas, or Florida as an employee or subcontractor of a Facebook vendor within a stipulated time period. The parties ultimately settled for $52 million and an agreement that Facebook would require all US vendors to implement a series of interventions designed to promote content moderators' wellness. These interventions included retaining licensed mental health clinicians with familiarity with PTSD, conducting pre-screening and assessments during the recruitment and hiring processes, providing one-on-one coaching sessions within the first month of onboarding, making group wellness sessions available, providing clear guidelines for how and when content moderators may excuse themselves from a particular graphic content type, allowing moderators to be moved to an alternative work assignment, and providing access to Facebook's anonymous whistleblower hotline. The settlement also requires that Facebook "continue to roll out a suite of well-being preferences" that allow moderators to toggle on or off features for mediating their exposure to graphic content, including viewing images in black and white, blurring images, blocking faces, blurring video previews, auto-muting videos when they start, being able to preview videos with thumbnail images, and preventing automatic playback as a default. Given the public-facing nature of the settlement terms, it's likely such interventions will increasingly become an industry standard.

What wasn't covered by the settlement, however, but can make a big difference in the psychological well-being and effective functioning of teams, was the ongoing need for social media platforms to continue to diversify their workforces. This serves multiple purposes. First, diversity can improve detection of potentially harmful content because staff with an array of linguistic, cultural, and social knowledge have a greater reach of awareness and insight about distressing content and misinformation. As noted in Chapter 3, while we may all watch the same video, we don't *see* the same things. Our experience of content is deeply subjective. What triggers an older white man may not be the same as what triggers a young woman of color. What a native Spanish speaker may pick up can and may differ from someone who only speaks English, or speaks Spanish but doesn't understand regional differences, including slang.

Second, team diversity can improve empathy and deepen the sense of community and belonging among members of that team. Especially when it comes to identity – for example, when violence is directed at someone who looks like you or has had similar experiences – having people on your team or in your social circle who

---

[14] "Facebook Content Moderators' Safe Workplace Litigation: About the Case," Joseph Saveri Law Firm Website, available at: www.saverilawfirm.com/our-cases/facebook-content-moderators-safe-workplace-litigation (last visited July 9, 2022).

understand first-hand the effects of that exposure can have a significant protective effect on your emotional well-being. Several people we interviewed underscored the power of diverse communities.

As Simon-Thomas spoke with us, she mulled additional possibilities for enriching employees' relationships with the material. "Maybe have restorative circles as part of their job? What if three times a week the [moderators] sat together and talked about how they managed their edge moments, those moments when they started to feel hopeless or too distressed to move forward? Soldiers come back from war with a strong sense of familial relationships with their colleagues." This could be similar. She challenged companies to be more creative: "How can we create community in the face of things that are really hard about society and behavior?"

IMPROVING USERS' EXPERIENCES

In 2013, the American Psychiatric Association released the fifth edition of the Diagnostic and Statistical Manual of Mental Disorders (DSM) – a tool used by psychiatrists and psychologists to diagnose mental illness. The new edition included exposure to upsetting online information as a potential cause of secondary trauma. This most recent version of the DSM acknowledges that PTSD can result from exposure to "actual or threatened death, serious injury, or sexual violence in one (or more)" of several ways, including by "experiencing repeated or extreme exposure to aversive details of … traumatic events."[15] This includes exposure to graphic violence and other types of traumatic material that police officers or other first responders might confront – as well as that which may be encountered online. However, as mentioned in Chapter 2, the guidelines only recognize the risk of PTSD in those who work with graphic material in a professional setting, leaving out the potential risk to everyday social media users, and explicitly omitting "exposure through electronic media, television, movies, or pictures, unless [the] exposure is work related."[16]

According to Frank Ochberg, who analyzed the DSM-5 drafting process, this was a conscious choice on the part of those tasked with updating the manual. The drafters felt it was important to exclude digital "ambulance chasers," those who spend hours online searching out graphic material – but notably, this can also include, for example, students or citizen volunteers looking into human rights violations. While the DSM's 2013 update marks an initial, official, and important recognition that those whose professions require spending hours online exposed to such content can suffer significant mental harms from that exposure, there was widespread sentiment among those familiar with the DSM that the potential pool of people who may suffer adverse outcomes from exposure to graphic content is

---

[15] DSM V Exhibit 1.3–4(B).
[16] DSM V Exhibit 1.3–4(B) (emphasis added).

much greater than the policy acknowledges. Many argued that the DSM should reflect that fact.

Social media companies can also make use of automation to help minimize exposure. As mentioned above, recent advances in artificial intelligence, especially machine learning processes that allow for automated object detection (of weapons, tanks, even blood and bullet wounds) and natural language processing that helps automate detection of online bullying, hate speech or other problematic phrasing, are making the widespread detection of potentially distressing content possible. AI is already being widely deployed for these purposes by many companies and promises to help companies scale future interventions.

Automation can also help detect information that violates companies' community rules due to its graphic nature. Identifying graphic posts is an ideal task for automation because algorithms don't get PTSD. However, automation can be a crude tool; as has been repeatedly demonstrated in the Syrian context, companies fumbled their first forays into automated take downs, often removing graphic information with legitimate news or human rights value.[17] There's a real danger in both allowing too much to stay up *and* taking too much information down. Ultimately, since reactions to content can differ so much from one individual to the next, it's incredibly important to find ways to increase users' control over what they see, when, and how.

Equally important is maximizing options for users' engagement. In 2017, several of the major tech companies – including Microsoft, Facebook, YouTube, and Twitter – banded together to create the Global Internet Forum to Counter Terrorism, otherwise known by the acronym GIFCT.[18] The forum was established to increase communication among the companies about terrorist content posted to their platforms and improve response times for detecting and removing such posts in order to minimize the harmful content to which users are exposed. Whenever one member of the forum detected such content, they would create what's known as a "hash" value – a string of letters and numbers that is unique to a particular digital item. When run across platforms' datasets, the hash value can be used to find other copies of that content. Each company would put hashes of terrorist content into the GIFCT repository, so that string of letters and numbers could be used by other companies to automate detection and removal of that item if also posted on their platforms. In this way, content could be removed from public view, protecting people from the potentially negative psychosocial impact of viewing terrorist content, whether that impact was pressure toward recruitment or psychological harm from viewing extrajudicial killings or hearing upsetting audio, while generating a log of hashes that could be shared with law enforcement.

[17] Avi Asher-Schapiro, "YouTube and Facebook Are Removing Evidence of Atrocities, Jeopardizing Cases against War Criminals," The Intercept, November 2, 2017.
[18] GIFCT Global Internet Forum to Counter Terrorism, "Story," available at: https://gifct.org/about/story/#june-26–2017—formation-of-gifct (last visited February 18, 2022).

One limitation of this repository, however, is that all that is contributed to the consortium is the hash value for each item, not the item itself, meaning that this system is created for detection but not for preservation of potentially helpful evidence of criminal acts. In parallel with GIFCT's creation, human rights and international criminal law experts have been calling for an international "evidence locker" for graphic content that companies need and want to remove from public view but that has potential evidentiary value for atrocity cases.[19] With such an evidence locker, companies could remove content from view but preserve that content for those who need it.

The international criminal law community first experimented with a type of centralized evidence collection for the conflict in Syria and separately for the conflict in Myanmar, creating what are known as "international, impartial mechanisms" for evidence preservation, aggregation, and analysis.[20] The idea behind those global experiments is that people, organizations, and governments around the world could contribute relevant data to the mechanisms, which would then preserve and process the data and later share the data with prosecutors who may come calling. These organizations were created to solve several problems: First, companies' desire to rid themselves of the content, despite their recognition that it might have critical value for later legal processes; second, to improve the evidentiary foundations of often quite difficult to prosecute international crimes and human rights violations; third, to ensure that witnesses and fact-finders had alternate places to send content, other than social media platforms, which were never designed to be evidence collectors in the first place (and thus are a poor fit for that purpose); and fourth, to deal with the time-lapse problem, where individuals are posting information about atrocities in close to real time, but cases may take months to years to build, with long lags before law enforcement organizations request preservation or production of content related to international and domestic crimes – giving perpetrators ample time to remove incriminating posts. These two mechanisms are somewhat limited, however, given that they are each conflict specific – to Syria and Myanmar, respectively – leaving digital evidence of thousands of atrocities from elsewhere around the world without a potential home.

Given the relative success of the Syria and Myanmar experiments, a number of organizations are now developing options for creating a system that could be used

---

[19] See, eg., Alexa Koenig, "Big Tech Can Help Bring War Criminals to Justice: Social Media Companies to Preserve Evidence of Abuse," *Foreign Affairs*, November 11, 2020; Alexa Koenig et al, *Digital Lockers: Archiving Social Media Evidence of Atrocity Crimes* (Human Rights Center 2021); Belkis Wille, *Video Unavailable: Social Media Platforms Remove Evidence of War Crimes* (Human Rights Watch 2020); Stephen Rapp, Federica D'Alessandra and Kirsty Sutherland, "Anchoring Accountability for Mass Atrocities: Providing the Permanent Support Necessary to Fulfill International Investigative Mandates," *OpinioJuris* (2020) (series covering the effort to identify and create political will for a conflict-agnostic repository for digital evidence of atrocities).

[20] For an overview of the mechanisms and their importance to international evidence collection, see Beth Van Schaack, *Imagining Justice for Syria* (Oxford University Press 2020).

for almost any conflict.[21] This system would centralize evidence collection for mass atrocities, creating new efficiencies with how such information is organized, preserved, deduplicated, tagged, coded, verified, and packaged for downstream international and domestic cases. It would also allow for streamlined communications with the major social media platforms, which could negotiate and share removed data with this new mechanism, instead of with the hundreds of smaller archives that are attempting to fill the void. While several of these platforms are incredibly powerful and critical to the effective functioning of justice, they could then focus on ensuring that the history of atrocities stays in the control and range of access of those who need it, as opposed to shouldering the often daunting costs of adequate server space required by long-term preservation, and the digital security needs that come with holding data that powerful government actors may want to have disappear.

Another concern is the privacy of platform users, who may have never intended that their content be used as evidence – for example, if something they posted becomes key evidence in a case and thus reaches audiences they never intended to reach. However, a potentially straightforward intervention would be to provide some way for users to indicate that they agree to have their content contributed to an evidence repository. In this way, users could indicate their consent (minimizing privacy concerns), retaining greater control over the end uses of their information, and simplify detection by platforms.

Even if this proposed system allows for social media platforms to more efficiently remove upsetting content but ensures it remains available for later justice and accountability, distress can come not just from the *content* of visual and written material but also from the *types* of engagement those posts attract, such as trolling – the online harassment of people that's designed to inspire an emotional response. In 2021, YouTube tweaked its use of the "dislike" button. While it technically retained the button, it hid "dislike" counts from viewers, in order to minimize the risk of bullying, especially coordinated attacks on disfavored posts, and purportedly to make their online spaces more positive.[22] However, many users protested because the dislike button had become a critical tool for critiquing and providing feedback to companies and others, and thus for quality control: For example, calling out corporations that bury ads in their programming on YouTube Kids (where ads are forbidden) or spotlighting those that spread disinformation. Ultimately, such modifications to the available response options could become finer grained. For example, instead of tying like and dislike buttons to particular *kinds* of accounts, social

[21] See, for example, Federica D'Alessandra, Sareta Ashraph, Stephen Rapp, and Kirsty Sutherland, *Anchoring Accountability for Mass Atrocities* (Blavatnik School of Government and University of Oxford 2022). At the time of writing, UC Berkeley's Human Rights Center staff are working with the Oxford Programme on International Peace and Security at the Institute for Ethics, Law and Armed Conflict at the University of Oxford, and the International Bar Association to advance this effort.

[22] YouTube Creators, "Update to YouTube's Dislike Count," November 10, 2021, available at: www .youtube.com/watch?v=kxOuG8jMIgI.

media companies could (and in our opinion, should) transfer control to the poster, allowing the poster to determine the kinds of feedback they'd find most helpful, in that way empowering posters to limit abuse, with perhaps an exception for private companies that may need the negative feedback, as a form of consumer protection.

Ultimately, content moderation isn't just a binary: keep up or take down. Companies can and do build in a spectrum of response options. For example, companies can use algorithms to deprioritize potentially harmful or distressing content, essentially erasing the likelihood that the everyday user will ever stumble upon that content but allow researchers and media to access the information by its URL. Some information may be useful, for example, to those seeking accountability for human rights or civil rights abuses; in such cases, de-prioritizations allow war crimes investigators, human rights activists, and others to also preserve and use the material as part of the process of seeking justice and accountability. Companies can also use algorithms to promote socially beneficial material, optimizing for users' mental well-being, instead of leveraging scandals to attract eyeballs.

In addition to helping identify graphic material, automated systems can be designed to slow people down from reflexively forwarding and reposting potentially damaging content. Some platforms have started using notices that ask users to consider whether they really do want to share content, when (for example) the credibility of the post's content has been called into question. This is a practice that could be considered for especially graphic material that doesn't violate a company's terms of service or community guidelines but comes dangerously close to that edge – or may for some subcategories of users.

Another relatively straightforward intervention is to warn potential viewers about what they're about to see. In Chapter 3, NYU Law Professor Meg Satterthwaite discusses the need for people to communicate what kinds of content they're sharing when passing along information that may be upsetting. The institutional, automation-driven parallel to this is to attach flags and other warnings, including those that temporarily block exposure to graphic content and require users to click their assent before accessing the content. Several platforms have already deployed such "click-through" warnings, which may increasingly become an industry norm. The archivist Eileen Clancy shared an example: By 2021, even CNN was embracing the practice of warnings and click-throughs. They prefaced a visual report on an August 2021 attack at the Kabul airport in Afghanistan that killed more than 180 people with a black screen. White letters read: "This story contains video and images viewers may find distressing." Then two options boxed in red: "enter with sound" and "enter without sound." Unfortunately, the post had a slightly grayed-out print that read "Best experienced with sound turned on" (something we would usually caution against) and failed to alert members of the public as to why they might want to enter with the sound off, but at least the precedent of a warning and click through was set.

Though automation is becoming increasingly involved in content moderation, human beings will always need to be part of the process in order to help with nuance and context and to aid as a check with the machines get things wrong. Moreover, some tactics that work with adults – such as printed warnings – may actually backfire for younger people who are drawn to looking at what they are warned against. One teenager we interviewed told us that he intentionally clicked on a video that showed a live-streamed suicide, after the warning provoked his curiosity. Algorithms are just no match for human creativity and understanding of nuance or context.

Given humans' exposure to graphic content, we should also all be thinking through how to strengthen education in ways that would empower users to improve the quality of their interactions online. This education should include a focus on (1) how to view graphic content to best protect oneself (as outlined in the "tips and tricks" section of Chapter 4); and (2) what to share, with whom and when, in order to better protect others (for example, with whom we vent online, or thinking through how to be considerate when forwarding content).

CREATING A NEW "PRO-SOCIAL" VISION

The Greater Good's Emiliana Simon-Thomas has had numerous opportunities to observe how online experiences can affect well-being, in the general sense of how people use their time on and offline, and how such patterns affect their thoughts and interpersonal behavior. In the early 2000s, Simon-Thomas was brought to Facebook by an engineer who was concerned with how to handle contentious posts, including graphic content related to human rights violations. At the time the team at Facebook was maybe a couple dozen people sitting in a room, deliberating about what should come down and what should stay up, and who should decide or take action. What struck Simon-Thomas was that people weren't asking for help supporting either employees or users from potential psychological harm. Nor was she invited to talk about the mental consequences of repeated exposure to such content and how to minimize the harms through human and digital interventions, though she urged the team to also focus on these issues. Instead, Facebook, now Meta, wanted guidance on how to categorize and handle ambiguous content, the kind that fell on the border between clearly needing to be removed and potentially staying up. Simon-Thomas helped Facebook build processes to encourage members of Facebook to message with each other instead of just reporting their frustration to the company when confronted with upsetting content that apparently didn't violate Facebook's policies – for example, when someone was embarrassed by a photo that someone else posted.

Later, the company wanted Simon-Thomas's help expanding how users communicated about posts, for example, by creating a more emotionally rich set of emojis than existed previously, and by finding other creative ways to encourage engagement given that social media posts don't have as much nuance or detail as in-person communication. But what *Simon-Thomas* wanted to discuss went well beyond emojis. She wanted to talk about how to create a "pro-social" online culture, for example, one that discourages bullying through not just technical but normative interventions. "All of social media has decided to avoid those social norms that we have in the physical world. They've said free speech is so precious we don't need to have social norms. I don't buy that."

As Simon-Thomas explains, governments, companies, and users have multiple levers they can press to create and/or strengthen positive social norms in online spaces – ones that parallel the kinds of social norms that help to minimize negative behaviors in our offline world, such as treating others as one would want to be treated or avoiding racial and misogynistic rhetoric. Just as humans generate social norms in all of the spaces they inhabit, companies can tweak their internal controls to optimize online norm building for the greater good. If they were to do so, social media companies might begin to fulfill their promise to "connect the world" in ways that strengthen the likelihood of true connection and minimize isolation – truly working for humanity's benefit.

Researchers at the Center for Humane Technology have been dogged in outlining how building a more pro-social online world could happen. According to their website, the center has a mission to "drive a comprehensive shift toward humane technology that supports our well-being, democracy, and shared information environment" by "radically reimagining our digital infrastructure."[23] This includes, at least in part, what kinds of content algorithms are used to prioritize and how content is policed more generally. As has been noted elsewhere, while companies like Meta/Facebook claim that more than 95 percent of the problematic content they remove from their site is identified by algorithms before a human ever sees that content, this percentage is misleading, given that all of the hateful content they remove may constitute "as little as 3–5% of hate [speech] on Facebook."[24] The Center for Humane Technology is determined to help ensure that fewer people are exposed to the remaining toxicity online.

Tristan Harris, one of the center's founders, was a design ethicist at Google when he released a presentation in 2013 titled "A Call to Minimize Distraction and Respect Users' Attention," which went viral. His proposal underscored how tech companies hijack peoples' attention in ways that are ultimately unhealthy, in part to make a fortune through advertising. He spotlighted how "successful products compete by exploiting [human] vulnerabilities," instead of helping people be more efficient and stress less. Describing the efforts of various social media companies as an "arms race to steal peoples' time" – from notifications that keep our phones buzzing to teasers about pictures that your friends have posted of you, he pointed out how the collective digital attack on our attention is ultimately "a tragedy of the commons that destroys our common silence and ability to think."[25] Harris ultimately underscored

---

[23] Center for Humane Technology, "Who We Are," available at: www.humanetech.com/who-we-are (last visited February 14, 2022).

[24] Keith Zubrow, Maria Gavrilovic and Alex Ortiz, "Whistleblower's SEC Complaint: Facebook Knew Platform Was Used to 'Promote Human Trafficking and Domestic Servitude,'" 60 Minutes Overtime, October 4, 2021.

[25] A concerned PM and entrepreneur, "A Call to Minimize Distraction & Respect Users' Attention," available at: www.minimizedistraction.com/.

that consumers, in effect, trust big companies to make conscious decisions "since they choose the systems. ... that control their lives."[26] He called on Google to create a team that would "standardize ... design ethics and define best practices to minimize distraction."[27]

Harris was eventually joined by Guillaume Chaslot, an engineer, who was helping Google design the algorithms that push users to next videos, but was growing increasingly concerned about what the company was selecting for: not quality content, but content that would keep eyeballs on the platform as long as possible in order to drive advertising revenue, and thus prioritized particularly scandalous content, including large quantities of mis- and disinformation. Today, Chaslot is listed as among the centers' "allies, key advisors and community." He has also co-founded AlgoTransparency.org, which is dedicated to informing the public by exposing "the impact of the most influential algorithms" on YouTube, as well as some other platforms,[28] to show how their viewing choices are being manipulated and rarely in directions that are in their best interest.

Academics and politicians have also begun to demonstrate how companies can create more pro-social online spaces. One example is provided by Audrey Tang, who famously transitioned from "school dropout to hacker to the world's first transgender minister," becoming digital minister of Taiwan, with a mandate to help establish the state as "a global leader in digital democracy."[29] She has embraced this mandate, contemplating what makes for a "prosocial, civic infrastructure as opposed to an antisocial, private sector infrastructure."[30] As she explains, in comments that reflect what Simon-Thomas told us, the physical world and digital world are far less apart than many initially assume, sharing a lot of the same healthy and unhealthy behaviors: "Just the same as we have physical places for people to talk about politics in a structured way: a town hall, a park or a university, an academic setting [in online spaces] people have to shout and compete with alcoholic drinks, private bouncers, and so on, around them." She explains that just as occurs in physical spaces, people online create and use digital spaces according to their communication needs. Where Simon-Thomas and Tang are especially in sync is around the ways that norms of behavior emerge and can be influenced by companies.

Tang has underscored the competence needed to co-create the worlds we want to be part of online – worlds that could build off research like that summarized above and are designed to encourage meaningful connection and discourage the loneliness

---

[26] Ibid.
[27] Ibid.
[28] See, for example, algotransparency.org (last visited February 14, 2022). For disclosure: The authors both worked with the founders of AlgoTransparency on research through the Human Rights Center's Investigations Lab.
[29] Jonas Glatthard and Bruno Kaufmann, "'Humour over Rumour': Lessons from Taiwan in Digital Democracy," SWI swissinfo.ch, May 7, 2021.
[30] Ibid.

that research has identified can be the downside of our technology use.[31] According to the clinical social worker Sherry Amatenstein, the impact of social media on loneliness – specifically, whether it increases or abates loneliness – depends on how you use it. Loneliness can be mitigated when social media is used to create offline connections and add to the ways we already communicate with loved ones. By contrast, spending hours drifting around online in place of fostering deeper human connection can exacerbate "feelings of loneliness and inadequacy."[32]

Several studies have suggested those with low self-esteem may be the most vulnerable to chronic loneliness. One study of nearly 2,000 US adults found a correlation between frequency of social media use and self-perceived social isolation.[33] Unfortunately, the study's authors couldn't tease out whether it was a sense of isolation that drove people to use social media more than average, whether social media use may have exacerbated any sense of isolation, or whether there was an iterative effect. However, later research suggests it can be protective to limit social media use to thirty minutes a day, demonstrating "significant decreases in anxiety" just from increasing *awareness* of the amount of one's social media use.[34]

People all over the world are investigating the potential social benefits of social media, an area that deserves more attention. Egyptian human rights advocate Yara Sallam, for example, in an interview with Ghadeer Ahmed, who founded *Girl's Revolution* on Twitter and Facebook following the 2011 revolution in Egypt, asked, "Why do you use the Internet?" In response, Ahmed illuminated some of the ways that social media can amplify the views of those whose voices may be suppressed in the physical world: "I use the Internet because it makes [my activism] easier for me, and it's accessible to lots of girls when we talk about sensitive issues: such as bodily rights and sexuality. Not everyone can talk about these issues, and of course if I hold a board in the street that says 'My virginity is my right' or 'My hymen is mine,' I know what can happen to me. But I can open a discussion online, and people can follow, and fall asleep and wake up while they're still discussing it normally. And there are ideas that can find a space to exist, regardless of whether it's timely or not, or if it's on the political agenda or not, or whether people think it's important or not."[35]

Those with whom we spoke who had worked on content moderation recognized that setting consistent, clear policy is really difficult, but they also had helpful

---

[31] Ibid.

[32] Sherry Amatenstein, "Not So Social Media: How Social Media Increases Loneliness," Psycom, May 15, 2019.

[33] Brian A. Primack, Ariel Shensa, Jaime E. Sidani, Erin O. Whaite, Liu Yi Lin, Daniel Rosen, et al, "Social Media Use and Perceived Social Isolation among Young Adults in the U.S.," 53 *American Journal of Preventative Medicine* 1 (2017).

[34] Melissa Hunt, Rachel Marx, Courtney Lipson, and Jordyn Young, "No More FOMO: Limiting Social Media Decreases Loneliness and Depression," 37 *Journal of Social and Clinical Psychology* 751–768 (2018).

[35] Yara Sallam, "Taking the Girl's Revolution Online: Interview with Ghadeer Ahmed," GenderIT.org, September 17, 2017, available at: https://genderit.org/es/node/5000.

insights on how to juggle competing social interests – like freedom of expression versus security or privacy. "I don't have a panacea," said Scott, when asked about policy changes she would recommend. "Since I left the space, it's changed a lot. When I first worked [at YouTube] I advocated a lot for free expression and especially for graphic content to stay up if it was exposing a human rights atrocity. I think a huge thing that has changed is the ability to disseminate this content." Whereas initially, content was relatively tightly tethered to a post's creator, now posts that go viral often spread at a speed and scale that quickly distances the content from the creator and their original intent, meaning that such posts can be used in very different ways than originally intended.

Scott also noted the moral imperative that social media companies have to focus on *how* content is posted and thus to address problematic content before it ever hits the platform. She explained that there are a lot of signals that companies can use to determine when something should be kept up because it advances freedom of expression versus when a post exploits a dedication to freedom of expression for nefarious purposes. "If someone posts a [single] thing versus someone who is bulk posting material … that difference gives away a different intent … So many times I would see bulk posted graphic content that didn't sit well with me. [Versus] there's something powerful about seeing 'this is the original person who posted it and the words they said with it.'"

She continued: "I saw many videos from Syria, for example, where the person is speaking, saying I am so and so, I am in [city X], and it's posted by this person and it's *clear* that they want this graphic content to be seen. I think the ability to see that speaker and see those words, it really makes you think 'we really need to keep this up.'" She felt strongly that the apparent intent of the poster should be weighted heavily, and that their relationship to the material matters, with the first posting of something being far more powerful than the many reposts that accrue when something goes viral.

Scott also points out that not all users are treated the same. She recalls a time when YouTube was especially focused on removing terrorist content and explains how that began manifesting in racist ways. People who post to YouTube can eventually earn income from advertising attached to their posts; however "Arabic-speaking users weren't able to monetize [their postings] in the same way [as English creators] and they were getting censored more." Others have similarly pointed out how geography, race and ethnicity have produced very different effects online. Several people with whom we spoke talked about how inattentive many people are to who controls the dissemination of visual media – from journalists to social media platforms – and how the framing around those visuals is controlled, often reinforcing biases.

From a policy perspective, while the companies themselves are learning quite a bit about what may better protect the public as they experiment with various interventions, external researchers need greater access to corporate-held data for independent research and analysis. Such access is a critical next step to not only better understand the potential impact of such interventions but also to disseminate insights across the digital ecosystem and inspire new theorizing about what may encourage pro-social interactions online.

One person who has been putting a lot of thought into the policy implications of corporate behavior is Brandie Nonnecke, director of the CITRIS Policy Lab at UC Berkeley. She's been advocating for regulation of social media companies that would facilitate the responsible sharing of data with researchers, both for oversight of what's happening on those platforms and to improve the quality of social media based research.[36] As she noted in a *Science* article, she co-wrote with her colleague Camille Carlton, access to social media company data could help the world better understand what kinds of graphic content people are being exposed to, and how they react to that exposure. She and her colleague have called for researchers to have legal access to social media data that have been made compliant with data privacy laws and regulations in order to advance scientific knowledge and policymaking. Of course, companies have a number of incentives to withhold such data, which Nonnecke notes include "financial, reputation and privacy reasons." Nonnecke and Carlton, however, outline both the need for this kind of information sharing and how it might responsibly play out across the many pieces of legislation that are currently being proposed in the United States and Europe, including anonymization of sensitive data, investment in research infrastructures, and careful consideration as to how "researcher" is defined, and thus who should have access.

Mariana Jones also argued that the responsibility to craft a more positive future extends beyond the companies: "I actually want more – and especially private companies want more – guidance from government and local agencies. Yes, there's a responsibility that companies have, but *should* they be the ones [setting] the guidelines? That conversation is not being [had]. It is such a joke. People who are Congress members or in other high positions of power who I imagine are well educated, and have *advisors*, don't even have basic proficiency [in tech and how it works]. This is astonishing." She pauses before addressing her next comments to Congress. "Yes, there needs to be accountability here, but what about your accountability?"

Michael Shaw also emphasized the need for greater governmental oversight, condemning how the free market has been allowed to control decisions around the broadcasting of potentially harmful digital content. "In the past, for example, the FCC closely monitored what could circulate in the media." That included so-called equal time rules for political messaging, public service announcements, and restrictions on advertising products with the potential for harm or abuse. "Back in the day, restrictions against alcohol commercials or direct-to-consumer ads for pharmaceuticals were off limits. Today, with the profit motive and special interests driving decision making, it is a free-for-all."

---

[36] Brandie Nonnecke and Camille Carlton, "EU and US Legislation Seek to Open Up Digital Platform Data," *Science*, February 10, 2022.

NYU's Stern Center for Business and Human Rights has advocated for the US Congress to pass legislation that would expand the Federal Trade Commission's authority to include oversight of social media companies and to approach the poor-quality content pushed by the companies like it would any other unfair corporate practice. Per the Federal Trade Commission Act, an unfair act or practice is defined as that which "causes or is likely to cause substantial injury to consumers which is not reasonably avoidable by consumers … and not outweighed by countervailing benefits to consumers or competition."[37] In 2022, the Stern Center issued a compelling report arguing that FTC oversight should be expanded in order to reduce hate speech, misinformation, "incitement to political violence and other forms of harmful content spread by social media platforms."[38] Their recommendations to Congress were straightforward: (1) empower the FTC to enforce a new mandate that the companies maintain procedurally adequate content-moderation systems that conform with platform rules, (2) require transparency about how companies' algorithms "rank, recommend and remove content," (3) require social media companies to maintain searchable and comprehensive advertising libraries that include disclosure of who has funded each ad, (4) honor first amendment principles by walling the FTC off from content moderation decisions, including what content gets taken down and what stays up, and (5) amend existing federal law to exempt FTC enforcement actions from legislation that protects social media companies from liability for what people post on their sites.

What kind of governance of social media companies is most needed? Over their relatively brief time in existence, Facebook and other major tech companies have been described as everything from the digital equivalent of public utilities to town squares to publishers to quasi-governments. As pointed out in a thought-provoking talk by writer/artist Ingrid Burrington in 2018, the analogy people use to describe social media companies changes the policy options that are considered when deciding how to appropriately regulate them.[39] Both rights and responsibilities shift considerably depending on which analogy is adopted. If Facebook is a publisher, then liability protections provided in laws like Section 230 – which protects Facebook from liability for what users post by saying Facebook is not a publisher – are outmoded. If Facebook is a quasi-governmental entity, then the best model for shaping a future in line with democratic norms would be to think about how to craft a constitution and bill of rights in order to empower those who spend their time online, and to check the power of the "state."[40] If the source is a public utility, regulation

[37] Federal Trade Commission Act §6 5(a).
[38] Paul M. Barrett and Lily Warnke, "Enhancing the FTC's Consumer Protection Authority to Regulate Social Media Companies," NYU Stern Center for Business and Human Rights, February 2022.
[39] Ingrid Burrington, "Political Structures and Infrastructures," in *Hacking Politics: Symposium, Berkeley Center for New Media*, October 19, 2018.
[40] Alexa Koenig, "It's Complicated: Why #DeleteFacebook Is Bad for Human Rights – And What We Should Do Instead," Medium, April 9, 2018.

may be the best option to ensure nondiscriminatory dissemination of information in the public interest. Or are private companies that are producing a potentially dangerous product like tobacco companies of the nineteenth and twentieth centuries? If so, then information campaigns, based on marketing principles that influence consumer behavior, and corresponding government regulation and enforcement of that product's relationship to advertising, may be the most productive way forward for preventing widespread harm.

Regardless of the analogy used to describe social media corporations, however, academia also has a central role to play. Programs ranging from those in elementary schools to middle and high schools to universities to continuing education should be funded and otherwise supported to educate users to make healthy and discriminating choices for themselves, their families and communities online. Psychologist Michael Shaw lamented, "There are no resources to help people process those. It's just a firehose." Others discussed the importance of teaching an emerging generation how to process graphic and other upsetting online information. Jones framed this as a need to teach people how to become responsible "digital citizens."

While thoughtful use of tech has to start in peoples' earliest years given the ubiquity of our lives with technology today, there's also an often-overlooked need to educate older generations whose interaction with social media may be less intuitive – and who have been exposed to fewer opportunities to learn about how social media works, and the potential for manipulation, than kids going through middle school, high school, and college today. Unlike digital natives, these "digital immigrants" may actually be least prepared to identify disinformation and misinformation, and most likely to trust what they see in the media as based in fact. And they have the social power and financial resources to do real damage when their decision-making is based on bad information.

Tang, the digital minister of Taiwan, has also seen generational differences in the competencies needed to strengthen digital democracy. As she's noted, "More than a quarter of citizen initiatives in Taiwan are digital democracy platforms started by people under the age of 18."[41] She has stressed the importance of "lifelong learning, intergenerational solidarity, reverse mentoring, and making sure young people get to set the agenda, so that they feel included in democracy even before adulthood."[42] Like Simon-Thomas, Tang believes that norm building must play a critical role in making online spaces more pro-social, explaining that "when people have a clear idea of what's considered a norm, multinational social media companies which violate this norm will face a lot of problems. If there is no particular norm for a certain issue, for example, around campaign finance transparency, then, of course, social media companies can just ignore the state altogether."[43] When certain behaviors

---

[41] Glatthard et al, 2021.

[42] Ibid.

[43] Ibid. See also, "Voices of VR Podcast #789: Human Rights in the Metaverse: Brittan Heller on Curtailing Harassment and Hate Speech in Virtual Spaces," August 6, 2019.

become normative, laws become less necessary. She has also underscored the stakes: "What's viral is not necessarily toxic. But when it is toxic ... if you wait a week, even if you wait just one night, then the toxic memes have already entered peoples' long term memory."[44] Finally, she notes the ability to counter this toxic information, by stressing that when the toxic information is countered, quickly, with a funny response, "humor" can dominate "rumor," motivating people to share "something enjoyable, rather than something retaliatory or discriminatory."[45]

Ultimately, all generations and sectors of society need to turn, and turn quickly, to confront their own vulnerability to propaganda and misinformation, as well as their potential role in building our future digital worlds, worlds that are increasingly inextricable from our offline existences. We've been warned about the dangers of social media and the circulation of graphic online material. How will this be exacerbated as more and more people live more of their lives in virtual reality – three-dimensional simulated digital spaces that immerse us for a diversity of reasons?

Our virtual worlds bring with them many of the joys and struggles – even crimes – to which we're subject in the physical world. People have been assaulted in virtual reality since its existence; those assaults are gaining increasing attention with media coverage of the "metaverse"[46] – the virtual reality world that overlays our physical world, in which people increasingly work, play, have relationships, and which the company Meta (formerly Facebook) is aggressively advancing. As of early 2022, it was reported that a "virtual gang rape" had already occurred in the metaverse.[47] Anyone who suggests such violence is "surprising" or "new" or "unpredictable" is either naive or disingenuous, as those who work in tech and social justice can attest given how new technologies have often developed hand in hand with sexually explicit material and behaviors, and various forms of abuse. What will the dangers be when we no longer just look at videos and photos of atrocity but are digitally immersed in the violence? What will our lifelines, and our cultural norms, look like then?

There's much we can learn from our experience with social media, but we need those with technical skills and positions of advantage to listen to and work more closely with those in the social sciences and the humanities to join together to not just react to, but proactively design, a humane digital future – and identify what incentives can be baked into that design to compel compliance. Pulling from her work with social media companies and how information is curated, Simon-Thomas commented: "I've had multiple conversations with young tech dudes who just hide behind free speech, asking who am I to say anything about what another person is

---

44 Ibid.
45 Glatthard et al, 2021.
46 Tanya Basu, "The Metaverse Has a Groping Problem Already," *Technology Review*, December 16, 2021.
47 Theo Wayt, "Meta Adds 'Personal Boundary' to Metaverse after 'Virtual Gang Rape,'" *New York Post*, February 4, 2022.

allowed to say? I always respond, 'It's not you, it's the platform that creates a culture and an environment that helps people make decisions.' ... The mistake those guys make is not leveraging that innate human tendency to not hurt others' feelings and to design *for that*. Most humans, barring a mental illness, truly dislike causing mental suffering in others."

Simon-Thomas described related conversations with engineers "who are coming from a place of earnest and may be profiteering for their company, trying to leverage AI and machine learning to tailor peoples' experiences [online]. I have a poignant memory of a young man changing teams, he was originally on what was called the 'compassion' team and he moved to 'ads.' It is common in tech to just switch teams, to make lateral and horizontal moves. His interest was 'How can I take what I've learned on the compassion team about emotions to be better at getting people to click on ads?'" His question touched on one of the things that bothered her the most in her consultations with tech companies: "The algorithm that helps you choose an exercise regime will also be great for serving up provocative information about politics" and undermining democracy.

In one of our last interviews for *Graphic*, Mariana Jones perfectly summarized all that we had learned, ranging from the importance of being aware of our reactions to graphic content to the tips and tricks we can all use to minimize harm to the importance of community. She shared her suggestions for those who stumble on or find this content in order to minimize the harms of that exposure: "I would say first and foremost remember *you're a human*. Take the time to acknowledge what you just went through versus suppressing this in your mind." She also had advice for those who might be excited to take on a career battling abuse and cruelty through digital spaces as trust and safety officers or as content moderators, or even as investigative reporters or researchers: "The first and most important thing I would say is 'be ruthless in your prioritization,' meaning put yourself first in all of this, meaning [don't ignore it when] your inner being is questioning something. Listen to it."

For those who feel that looking at graphic content doesn't faze them, she begged them to ask, even if they think they're okay, "What brings joy to you? Don't lose those things. Find community, find people you can talk to." For those who review graphic content as part of their job, she warned that it's important to keep a written record of how long you want to do that work and stay accountable to that plan. She explained that it can be incredibly easy to fall into a cycle of always wanting to do more to help others, ignoring your own well-being in the process.

Jones, who had once studied governance, closed with a reflection on society more generally and how much or how little people should be exposed to what currently circulates online, asking a normative question: how aware should we all be of what's happening in this world? She underscored the pervasiveness of graphic, upsetting content. Social media isn't "even like the dark net. Honestly you can find this [graphic material] anywhere." She stressed the need to educate people on how to engage with such content, "on what it means to put someone's most vulnerable pain into something. Today, we focus for maybe two hours on an issue [like the killing of George Floyd] and then we move on. It's something I would love to spend more time thinking about. Should we have community standards about behavior online? The way I kind of see it is we need to have these standards and form some kind of contract about how to behave. In a digital world, these translate into community standards that you have to agree to before using a site. But most people don't read or engage with the standards. You create an account and quickly scroll all the way down, you don't read it, and you click ["agree"]. I think [these issues are] going to be even more important as we switch into virtual worlds, or the metaverse. So like, how do we think about that? The lack of education and awareness as digital citizens is … missing from the conversation."

* * *

The tragedy in Christchurch took place as we were writing the proposal for this book – a tragedy in which a perpetrator weaponized new technology in the form of livestreaming and leveraged a captive online audience to magnify the terror he hoped to spread by bringing it to millions across the globe. As we write these words, Facebook has just changed its name to Meta, preparing for the virtual reality–based future it believes is coming. Soon, whether we're ready or not, many of us will live, work, and play in parallel and interlocking worlds that will increasingly be recognized as one. It's up to all of us to figure out how we work together to keep everyone safe, and what we want those worlds to look like.

Afterword

Lessons on Resilience from San Miguel

When we began working on this book, we traveled to San Miguel de Allende, Mexico, to spend time with seasoned organizer, writer, and Human Rights Center board member Deborah Goldblatt. Goldblatt is an expert in the World Café method of community conversations and had previously directed the organization that sponsors that work globally. In order to help us probe the question of how to foster resilience to online depictions of trauma, Goldblatt organized a World Café–style event at Calle Recreo in San Miguel.

A World Café event goes something like this: Assemble people in an intimate, café-like environment and cover tabletops with butcher block paper and colorful pens. Welcome the guests, set some ground rules (what's said in the café stays in the café, talk but don't talk too much, phones off the table). Pose questions in twenty-minute rounds and allow participants to move to another table after each round but with one person remaining behind to anchor the table and describe highlights of the previous conversation. Finally, "harvest" each conversation for a discussion with the whole group.

Goldblatt invited fifteen women for conversation and maybe a mezcal or two. Among those who attended were a goat herder/cheese maker, filmmaker, restaurateur, designer, property manager, lawyer, artist, writer, trapeze artist, and telenovela actor. One woman was pregnant and another a grandmother. The group ranged in age from about twenty-five to seventy-five, the trapeze artist well into her forties. A third of the group were Mexican, almost half were American, two Brazilian, and one French Nicaraguan.

The first question put to the women: "What does resilience mean to you?" Handwritten words propped on cardboard on the bar offered an opening definition: "Resiliency: the ability to bounce back quickly." Our collective task: consider if this definition resonates. We took turns drafting personal definitions and sharing our words:

Resilience is a set of tools to help us overcome: these tools are determination, optimism, flexibility, humor.
Resilience is a process: it's like passing a "tope" (a speedbump) in that you have to slow down, move through it.

FIGURE C.1 Reflections about resilience from San Miguel de Allende, Mexico, in 2019. Source: Photo by Alexa Koenig

Resilience is a response to grief and suffering.
Resilience is not a one-time thing, but rather a mindset, a process.
Resilience is not about bouncing back, it's about bending.

Women picked up colorful markers and wrote words in every direction as the conversation unfolded, until the words made rainbows across the butcher paper, outlining what resiliency is and how to maximize it: reframe the future (Figure C.1). Cognitive flexibility. Alone? Analyze: Why am I in this position and how am I going to get out of it? Power. Empowerment. Self-care. Self-love. Elasticity. Faith. I am enough.

As we gathered insights for our book, we connected the dots from these personal experiences to our interface with collective trauma online. When we led the Investigations Lab, we were constantly working to better equip young adults to grapple with potentially difficult imagery of human suffering; to help them gather the tools necessary for handling the intense emotions that come from listening to a mother wailing in grief in the aftermath of a bombing, from reading hateful Facebook posts, from seeing a dead child; the incessant and often ahistorical stream of images of mass shootings, children kept in cages, ice caps melting, and the like, coupled with vitriolic and often violent rhetoric from leaders. We shared some of this work experience with the women in San Miguel and talked about the struggle to know when to look, to know when to look away, and what to do with what you see. How do we prepare human rights advocates to do this work for the long haul? How do we ensure *we* can do this for the long haul?

In response, a filmmaker – who had just made a documentary about the criminalization of midwifery in Mexico and the deaths of Mexican women in childbirth – had this revelation: "You're talking about resilience as a responsibility." Resilience as responsibility.

Indeed, the responsibility to be resilient (with and for others) binds this work as well as our obligation as global citizens to consume online information responsibly. While social media companies have a long way to go to help mitigate the potential harms of what users post to their platforms, it's also on all of us to know what we can do to keep ourselves, our families, and our friends safe – and even help them thrive online. And as people who care about our collective future, it's the idea that those with privilege can use that privilege to engage with suffering in pro social ways – even if the content is challenging or unsavory. To this end, people with privilege have a special responsibility to develop greater resilience given that an extraordinary burden has far too long fallen on people of color and other "historically resilient" communities.

So often in the United States, we hear people saying: "I just can't read the news anymore." It's from this place of privilege that some of us can choose to step back from world events when others cannot. Perhaps we shouldn't wholesale turn off the news and instead think about how to be healthier, more intentional, and more proactive in how we engage with the news – so that we actually can continue to engage in critical ways with the immense and urgent challenges of our times. Even if responsibility drives resilience, we don't have to emulate the tough-it-out, traditional style of old-school journalists and human rights workers. Resilience doesn't mean suck it up, drink until you're numb, eat poorly, or burn out in a blaze of self-congratulatory glory. It also doesn't mean to just do some down dogs or 5-minute meditations to offset the inequities in your office.

Resilience can be cultivated and practiced in a community of women in a mezcaleria in the middle of Mexico, or in a law school classroom, or in the belly of a tech company, or with a fellow investigator. It can be cultivated with our children, with our partners and our parents, with colleagues and even strangers.

Most importantly, we need to keep asking: How do we as a society make sense of and keep ourselves safe from the unprecedented onslaught of graphic imagery that is present in our daily lives? How do we become resilient and make space for restoration – a sense of returning to a baseline of well-being from which we can positively interact with others[1] – instead of being removed from life? How do we transition from our traumatic experiences to a state of post-traumatic growth? How do we teach our children to take in the cruelties of the world and confront those cruelties on and offline, without being overcome or hardened by them?

While the community and settings were different in San Miguel than in Berkeley and the subject matter more intensely personal than what we might confront at work, many of the emergent themes were spot on: the need to develop self-awareness and relevant tools, to call on community, to practice self-care, to engage and not avoid – but to consciously look away when that's what's needed – and to understand privilege and the power of privilege to engage and to make things better for others.

---

[1] For an overview of the role of restoration in mental well-being, see, for example, Nural Ain Nabilla Mohd Yusli, Samsilah Roslan, Zeinab Zaremohzzabieh, Zeinab Ghiami, and Noorlila Ahmad, "Role of Restorativeness in Improving the Psychological Well-Being of University Students," 12 *Frontiers in Psychology* (2021).

FIGURE C.2 Human Rights Center board member Deborah Goldblatt led a discussion on resilience in San Miguel de Allende, Mexico, which culminated in a birthday celebration for author Alexa Koenig, underscoring the importance of community and laughter to well-being.
Source: Photo by Andrea Lampros

It's our hope that these kinds of discussions, illuminated by research and practice – had by the women of San Miguel de Allende, by journalists and therapists, by students, by parents, by social workers and soldiers, and by first responders of all stripes – will lead to a new architecture for engaging with global violence and bearing witness in ways that are sustainable and healthy, both for this generation and generations to come.

At the culmination of our gathering, our host celebrated the fact that it was Alexa's birthday in a traditional Mexican way: Singing Féliz Cumpleaños and then promptly shoving her face into a pie made of whipped cream (Figure C.2). There in the mezcaleria, we may have found one of the most tried, true, and healthy resiliency tools, one that's born from community: laughter.

Note on Images, Identity, and Social Justice

Some fifteen unsanctioned graffiti artists converged on Pittsburgh's Allegheny riverfront around 4 am, just days after George Floyd's killing in 2020. Under cover of semi-darkness, the artists began painting the 12-foot words Black Lives Matter along with portraits of Floyd, Breonna Taylor, Pittsburgh teenager Antwon Rose II, and other Black victims of police violence. To obscure the illegality of their actions, the artists wore safety vests and peppered the area with safety cones, to suggest they were working on behalf of the city or under some other official sanction. One of the artists described the passionate early-morning convergence and collaboration as "a Paris Commune moment."

Days later, a Pittsburgh media outlet reported on the powerful artwork, mistakenly stating that the guerrilla artists were all white and that their work had been paid for and sanctioned by the city. While none of this was true, issues of intention, identity, and appropriation erupted in Pittsburgh and beyond – issues that are still playing out today. Some Black muralists criticized the alleged lack of inclusivity of artists of color, unaware that the original artist invited to work on the project, who is Black, had been unable to join. To explain why they proceeded anyway, the artists noted that creation of an illegal mural is risky. As stated by Max Gonzales, one of the original muralists, in Pittsburgh magazine, "We didn't want to get free labor from Black artists, [and] we didn't want to put Black bodies in harm's way. This was done by illegal graffiti artists and we've all been arrested and had our run-ins with the law. We didn't want to put Black bodies in the way of that." One of the original muralists, who is Black, said, "Painting a singular mural is never simple. It can get messier and messier." Art and life are intertwined and inextricable.

We took the photo of this mural in 2021 during a visit to Pittsburgh for a conference on hate; during a break, we wandered down to the Allegheny River to discuss the manuscript for our book. We did not know the backstory, but as soon as we stumbled across the mural we hoped to use the image on the cover of *Graphic* (which ultimately was not possible due to image resolution). The mural's many versions – its ephemerality and the ways it has prompted heated conversations around images and identity, much like the graphic digital content with which we have been grappling – attracted

us to it. How are images, such as the video of George Floyd's murder, taken by then-seventeen-year-old Darnella Frazier, or a mural painted by a collective in the dead of night, both catalysts for action? What violence and which victims do we see or not see? How does our own identity affect how we take in and interact with the pain and resilience of others?

While this particular iteration of the mural was subsequently painted over by a Black artist who *was* commissioned by the City, the conversation about the mural – about activism and justice – continues. When we spoke with the muralists who worked on this version to see if they were okay with us featuring their work, they explained how a painful process gave rise to rich discussions about race and identity as well as progress toward greater inclusion. The mural may no longer exist in this form, but the ongoing actions and goodwill of the Pittsburgh artists to collectively create something powerful – in art and life – endure. Ultimately, we could not use this as the cover image because the photograph was not high resolution enough, but we wanted to share this story.

Thank you to Pittsburgh artists Max Gonzales, Shane Pilster, Jerome Charles, and Brian Gonnella for sharing their experiences. To support the work of muralists and other artist collectives in Pittsburgh, please consider donating to the Hemispheric Conversations Urban Art Project at https://hcuap.com.

Suggested Reading

RESILIENCE IN HUMAN RIGHTS WORK

Brown, Adrienne Maree (2019). Pleasure Activism: The Politics of Feeling Good. AK Press.

Dubberley, Sam, Griffin, Elizabeth, and Bal, Haluk Mert (2019). Making Secondary Trauma a Primary Issue: A Study of Eyewitness Media and Vicarious Trauma on the Digital Frontline. Available at: http://eyewitnessmediahub.com/research/vicarious-trauma

Greater Good Toolkit: Science Based Practices for A Meaningful Life. Visit www.holstee .com/products/greater-good-toolkit.

Gupta, Nikita (2022). Promoting Restoration and Capacity Building for Human Rights Investigators. https://canvas.ucsc.edu/courses/51093

Lipsky, Laura van Dernoot (2018). The Age of Overwhelm. Berrett-Koehler Publishers.

Nagoski, Emily and Nagoski, Amelia (2019). Burnout: The Secret to Unlocking the Stress Cycle. Ballantine Books.

Remen, Rachel Naomi (1997). Kitchen Table Wisdom: Stories That Heal, 10th Anniversary Edition Paperback. Riverhead Books.

Seligman, Martin E.P. (2011). Flourish: A Visionary New Understanding of Happiness and Well-being. Atria Paperback.

OPEN SOURCE INVESTIGATIONS

Dubberley, Sam, Koenig, Alexa, and Murray, Daragh (2020). Digital Witness: Using Open Source Information for Human Rights Investigation, Documentation, and Accountability. Oxford University Press.

Hill, Marc Lamont and Brewster, Todd (2022). Seen & Unseen. Atria Books.

Murray, Daragh, McDermott, Yvonne, and Koenig, Alexa (2022). Mapping the Use of Open Source Research in UN Human Rights Investigations. Journal of Human Rights Practice. 14(2): 554–581. https://doi.org/10.1093/jhuman/huab059

Otis, Cindy L. (2020). True or False: A CIA Analyst's Guide to Spotting Fake News. Feiwel and Friends.

IDENTITY AND TECHNOLOGY

Benjamin, Ruha (2019). Race after Technology: Abolitionist Tools for the New Jim Code. Polity.

Noble, Safiya Umoja (2018). Algorithms of Oppression: How Search Engines Reinforce Racism. New York University Press.

Richardson, Allissa V. (2020). *Bearing Witness While Black: African Americans, Smartphones, and the New Protest #Journalism*. Oxford University Press.

PLATFORM GOVERNANCE

Kaye, David (2019). *Speech Police: The Global Struggle to Govern the Internet*. Columbia Global Reports.
Roberts, Sarah T. (2021). *Behind the Screen: Content Moderation in the Shadows of Social Media*. Yale University Press.

SCIENCE

Herman, Judith (1992). *Trauma and Recovery: The Aftermath of Violence – From Domestic Abuse to Political Terror*. Basic Books.
McNally, Richard J. (2003). *Remembering Trauma*. The Belknap Press of Harvard University Press.
Mollica, Richard F. (2006). *Healing Invisible Wounds: Paths to Hope and Recovery in a Violent World*. Vanderbilt.
O'Keane, Veronica (2021). *A Sense of Self: Memory, the Brain, and Who We Are*. W. W. Norton & Company.
Sapolsky, Robert M. (2017). *Behave: The Biology of Humans at Our Best and Worst*. Penguin.

PHILOSOPHY AND MEDIA

DiIgnazio, Catherine and Klein, Lauren. *Data Feminism*. The MIT Press.
Sontag, Susan (2003). *Regarding the Pain of Others*. Picador.

Printed in the United States
by Baker & Taylor Publisher Services